LEONARDO
DA VINCI

BY DIEGO AGRIMBAU   ILLUSTRATED BY DIEGO ABALLAY

CAPSTONE PRESS
a capstone imprint

Graphic Library is published by Capstone Press,
1710 Roe Crest Drive, North Mankato, Minnesota 56003
www.mycapstone.com

Cataloging-in-Publication Data is available on the Library
of Congress website.
ISBN 978-1-5157-9163-8 (library binding)
ISBN 978-1-5157-9167-6 (paperback)
ISBN 978-1-5157-9171-3 (eBook PDF)

Summary: Follow the life of Leonardo da Vinci as he goes
from student to master painter in this unofficial biography.

Author: Diego Agrimbau
Illustrator: Diego Aballay

Translated into the English language by
Trusted Translations

Printed in the United States of America.
010370F17

TABLE OF CONTENTS

CHAPTER I
THE MADONNA OF THE CARNATION

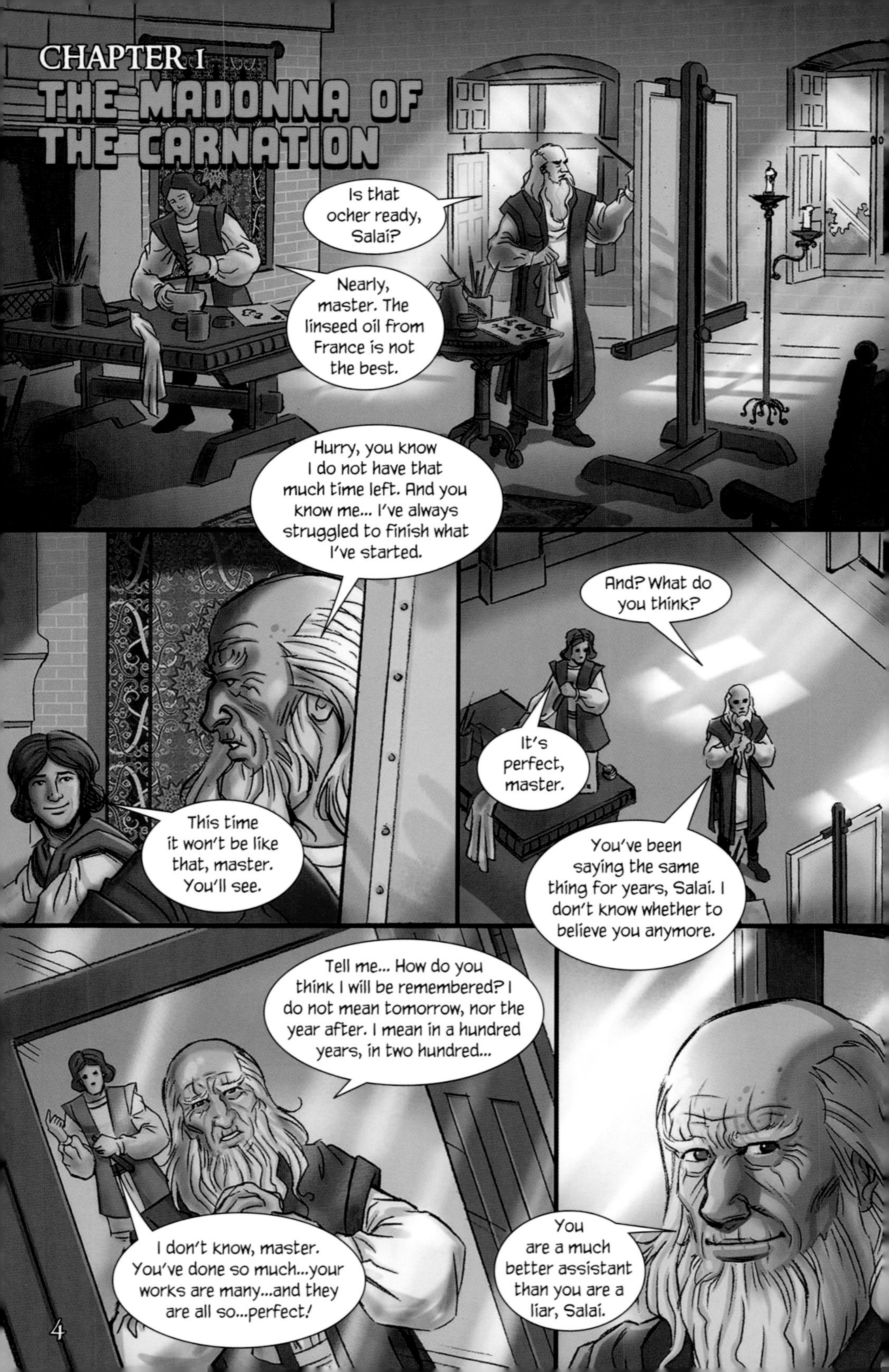

Is that ocher ready, Salai?
Nearly, master. The linseed oil from France is not the best.
Hurry, you know I do not have that much time left. And you know me... I've always struggled to finish what I've started.
This time it won't be like that, master. You'll see.
And? What do you think?
It's perfect, master.
You've been saying the same thing for years, Salai. I don't know whether to believe you anymore.
Tell me... How do you think I will be remembered? I do not mean tomorrow, nor the year after. I mean in a hundred years, in two hundred...
I don't know, master. You've done so much...your works are many...and they are all so...perfect!
You are a much better assistant than you are a liar, Salai.

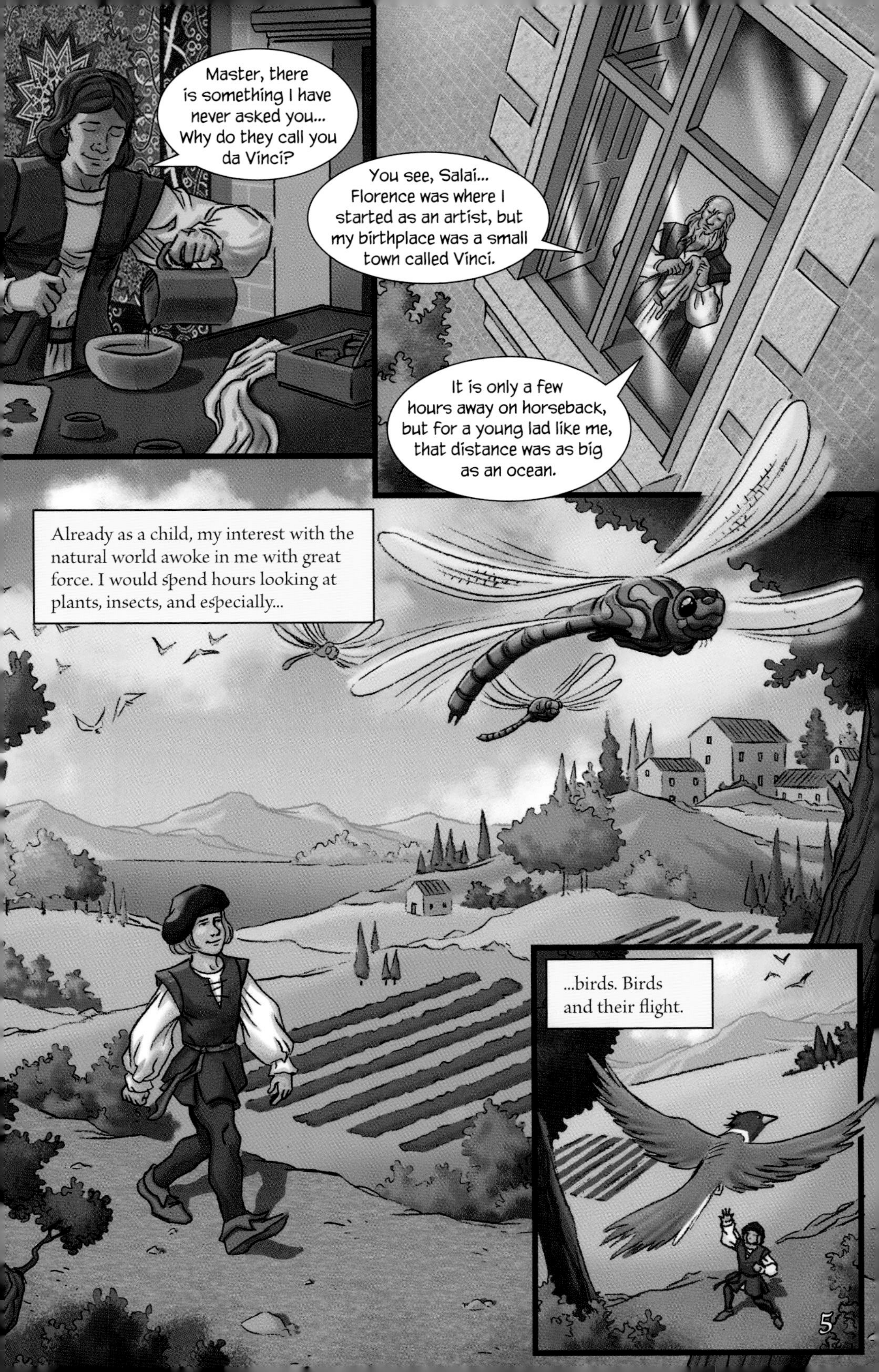
Master, there is something I have never asked you... Why do they call you da Vinci?
You see, Salai... Florence was where I started as an artist, but my birthplace was a small town called Vinci.
It is only a few hours away on horseback, but for a young lad like me, that distance was as big as an ocean.
Already as a child, my interest with the natural world awoke in me with great force. I would spend hours looking at plants, insects, and especially...
...birds. Birds and their flight.

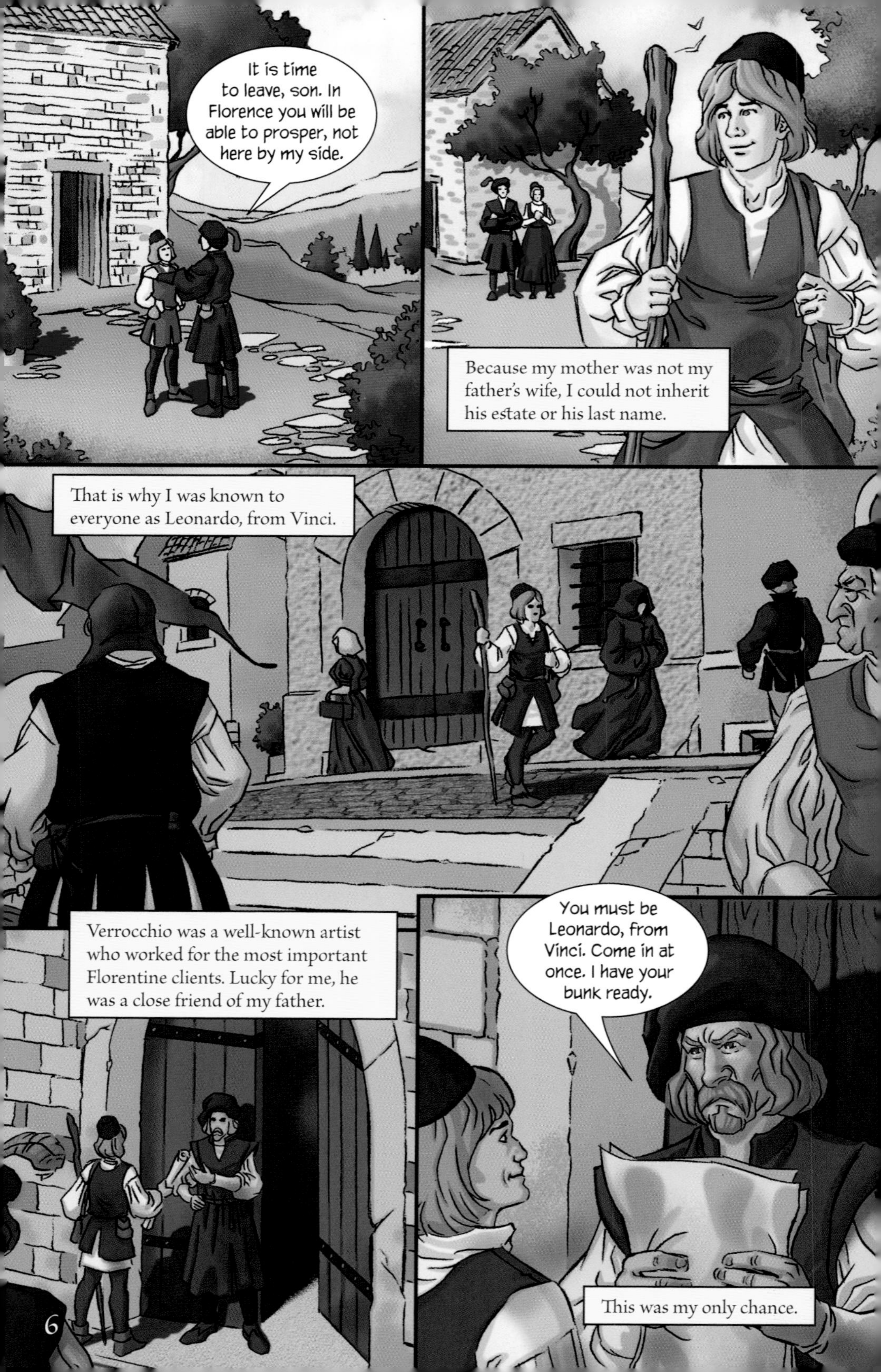

It is time to leave, son. In Florence you will be able to prosper, not here by my side.
Because my mother was not my father's wife, I could not inherit his estate or his last name.
That is why I was known to everyone as Leonardo, from Vinci.
Verrocchio was a well-known artist who worked for the most important Florentine clients. Lucky for me, he was a close friend of my father.
You must be Leonardo, from Vinci. Come in at once. I have your bunk ready.
This was my only chance.

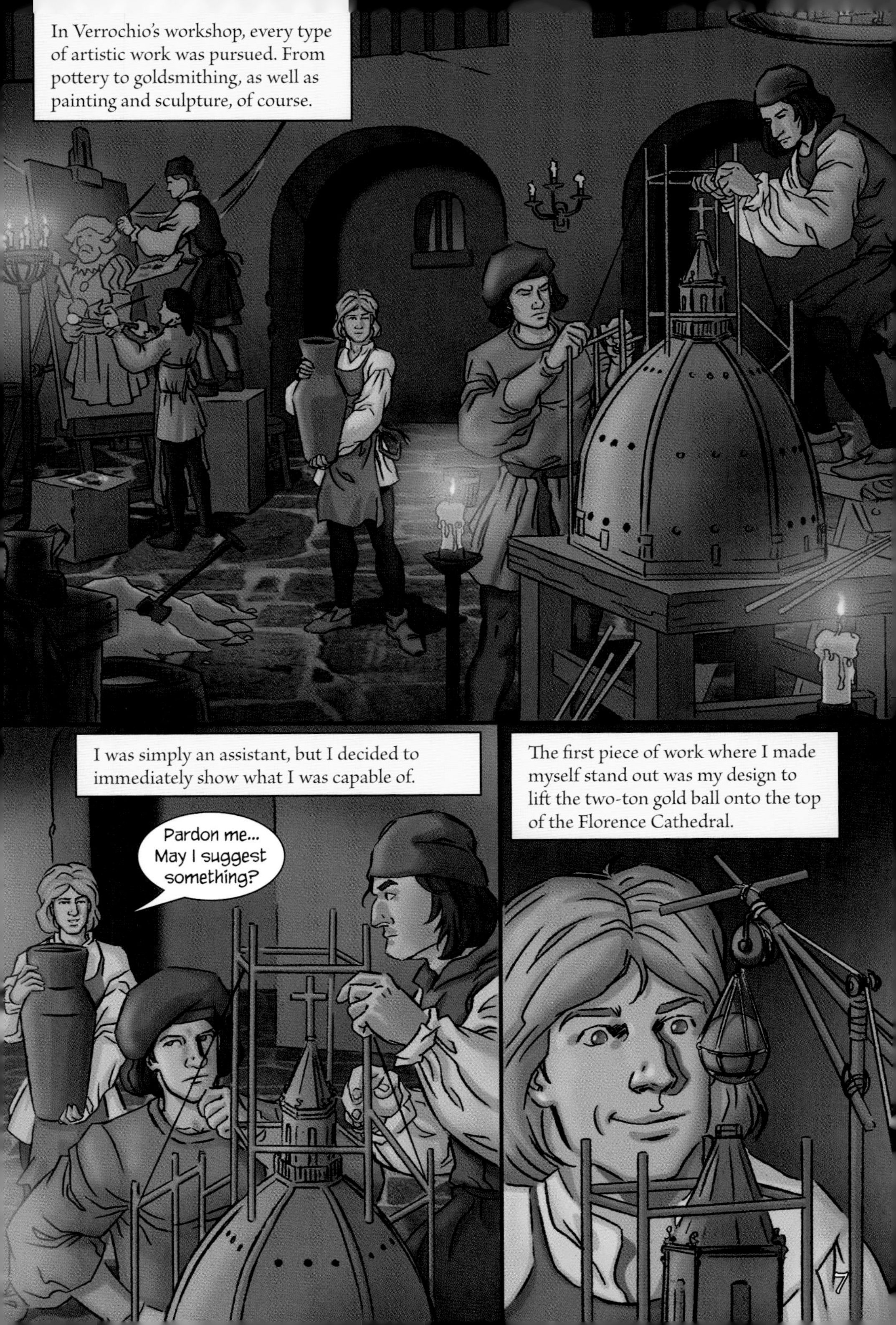
In Verrochio's workshop, every type of artistic work was pursued. From pottery to goldsmithing, as well as painting and sculpture, of course.
I was simply an assistant, but I decided to immediately show what I was capable of.
Pardon me... May I suggest something?
The first piece of work where I made myself stand out was my design to lift the two-ton gold ball onto the top of the Florence Cathedral.

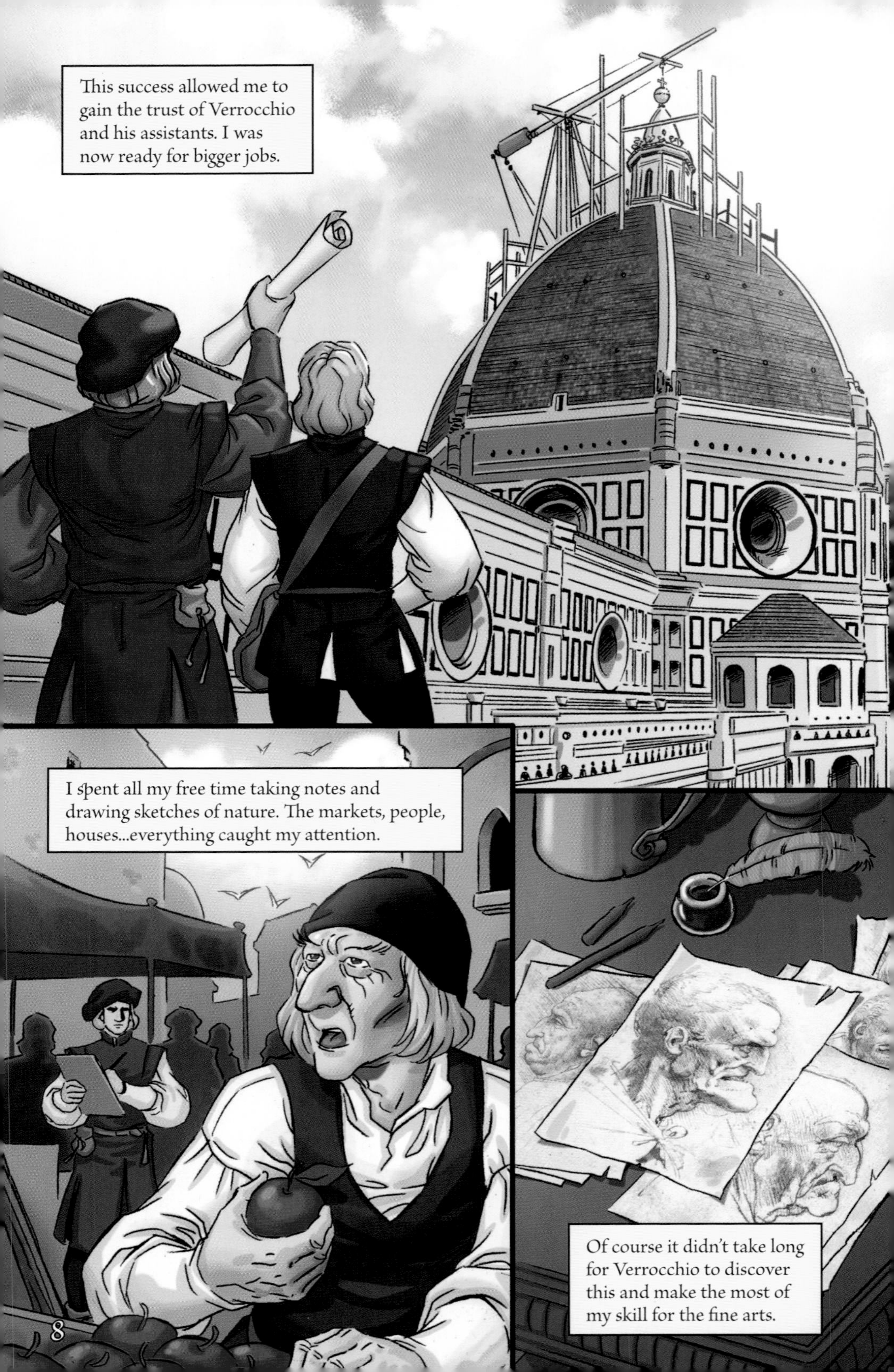
This success allowed me to gain the trust of Verrocchio and his assistants. I was now ready for bigger jobs.
I spent all my free time taking notes and drawing sketches of nature. The markets, people, houses...everything caught my attention.
Of course it didn't take long for Verrocchio to discover this and make the most of my skill for the fine arts.

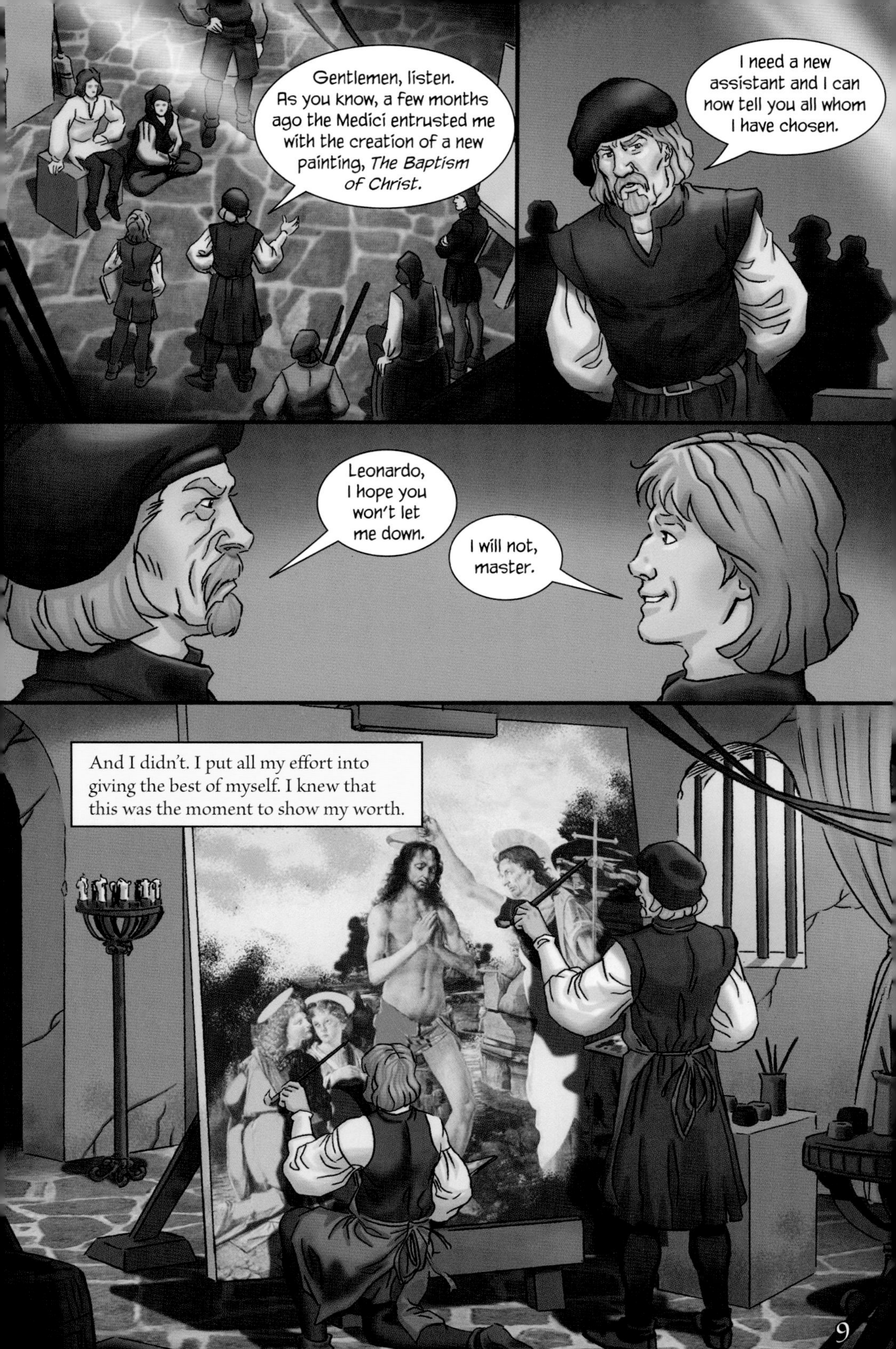
Gentlemen, listen. As you know, a few months ago the Medici entrusted me with the creation of a new painting, *The Baptism of Christ*.
I need a new assistant and I can now tell you all whom I have chosen.
Leonardo, I hope you won't let me down.
I will not, master.
And I didn't. I put all my effort into giving the best of myself. I knew that this was the moment to show my worth.

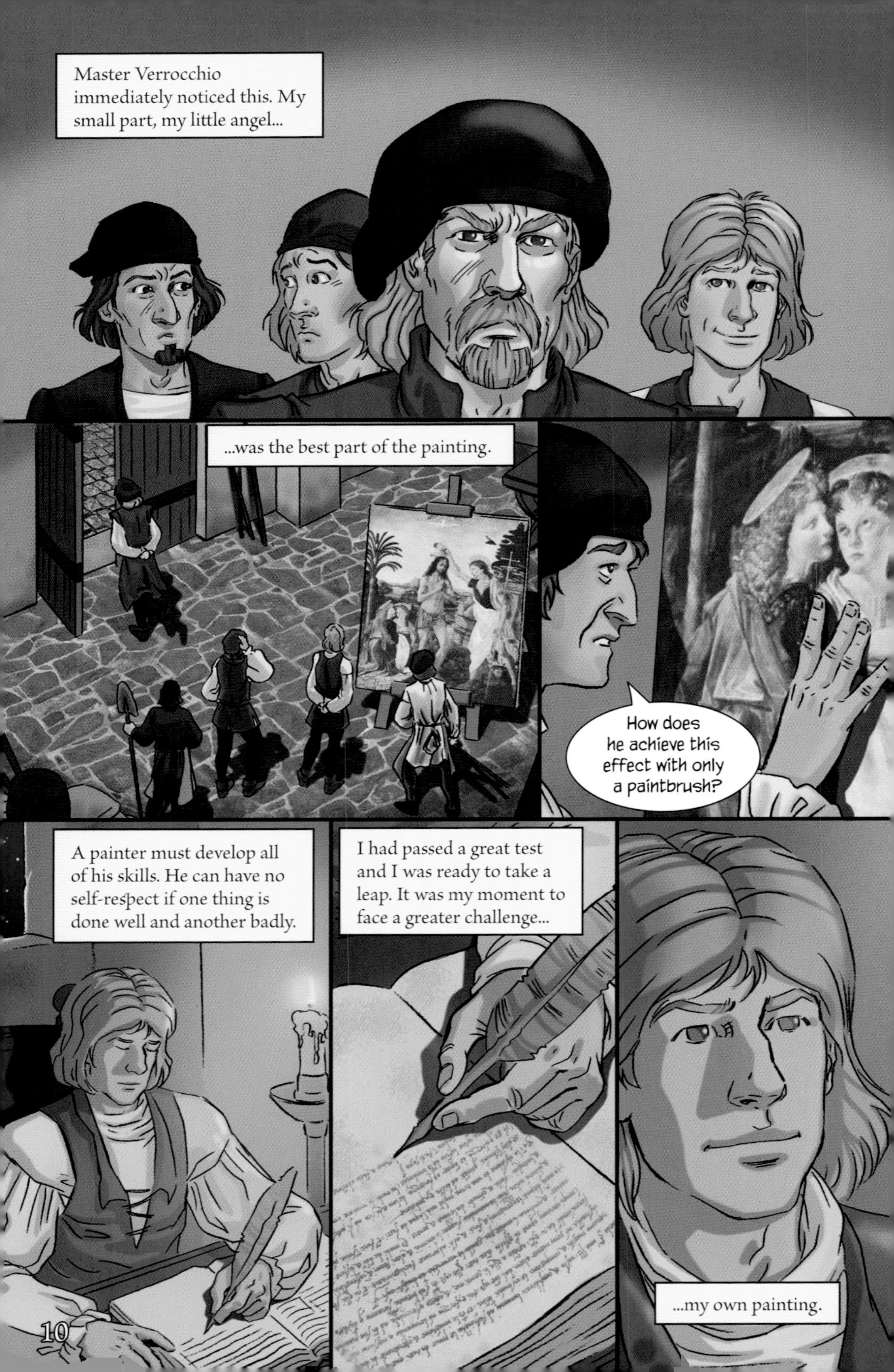
Master Verrocchio immediately noticed this. My small part, my little angel...
...was the best part of the painting.
How does he achieve this effect with only a paintbrush?
A painter must develop all of his skills. He can have no self-respect if one thing is done well and another badly.
I had passed a great test and I was ready to take a leap. It was my moment to face a greater challenge...
...my own painting.

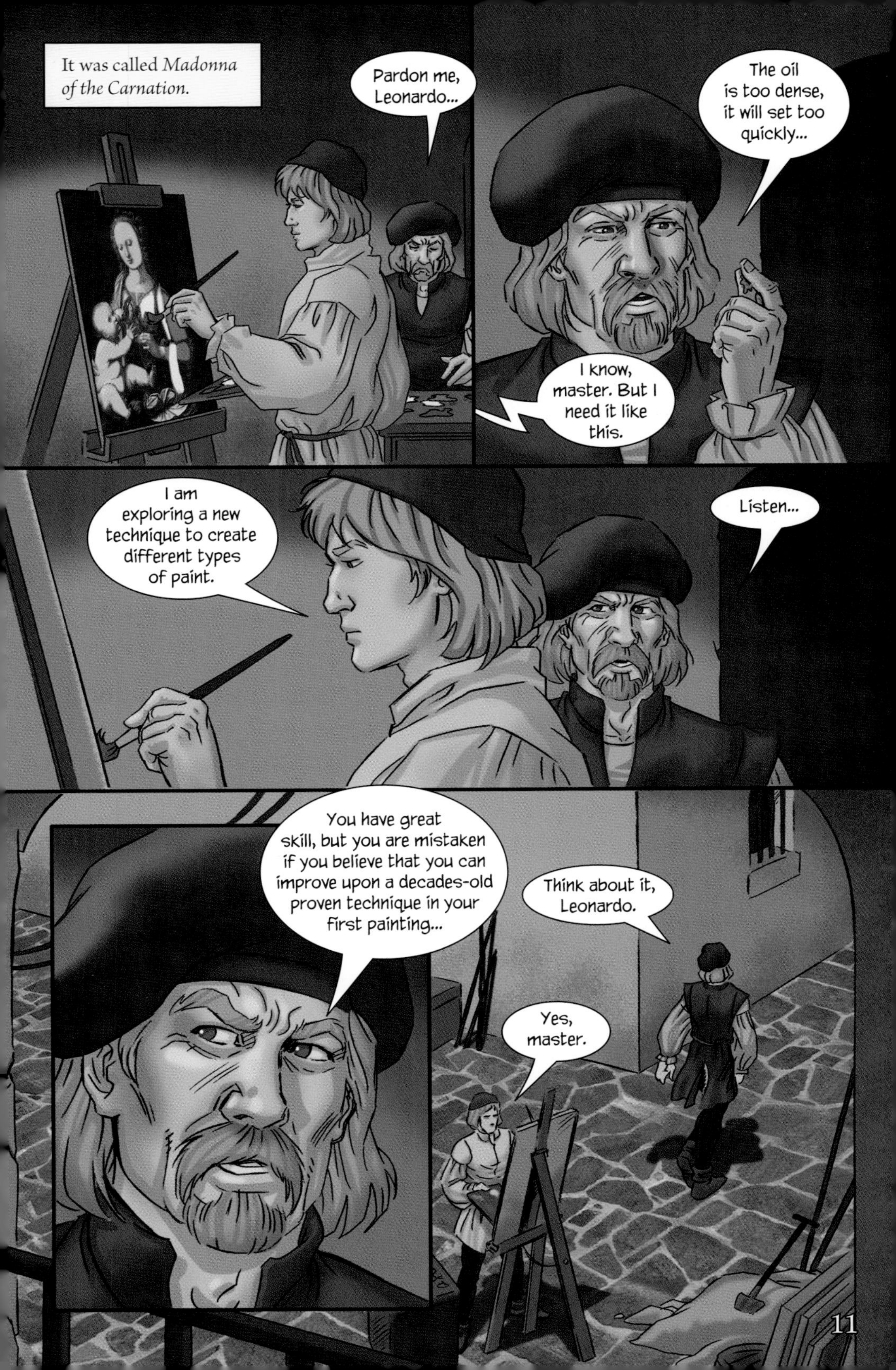
It was called *Madonna of the Carnation.*
Pardon me, Leonardo...
The oil is too dense, it will set too quickly...
I know, master. But I need it like this.
I am exploring a new technique to create different types of paint.
Listen...
You have great skill, but you are mistaken if you believe that you can improve upon a decades-old proven technique in your first painting...
Think about it, Leonardo.
Yes, master.

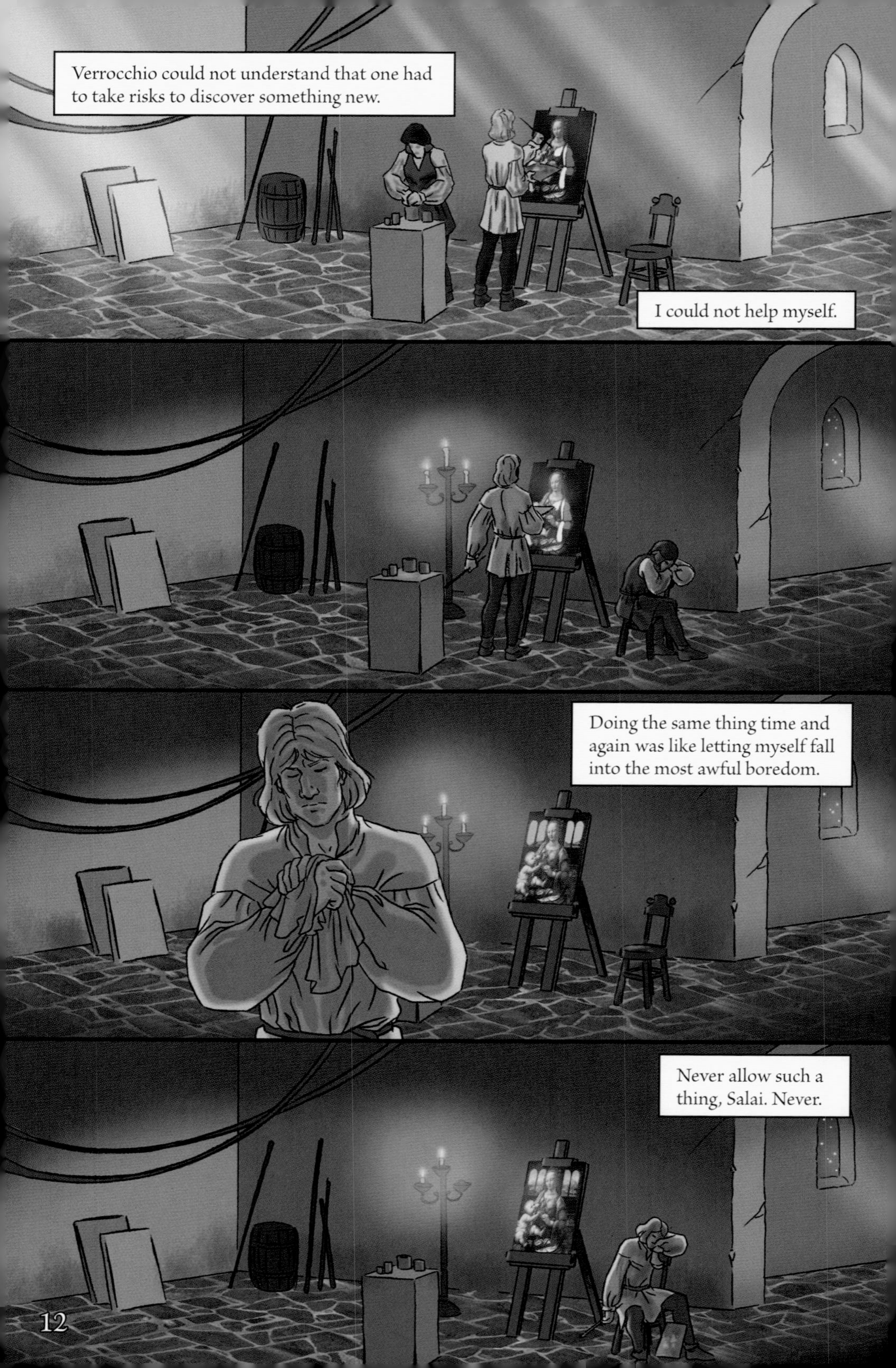
Verrocchio could not understand that one had to take risks to discover something new.
I could not help myself.
Doing the same thing time and again was like letting myself fall into the most awful boredom.
Never allow such a thing, Salai. Never.

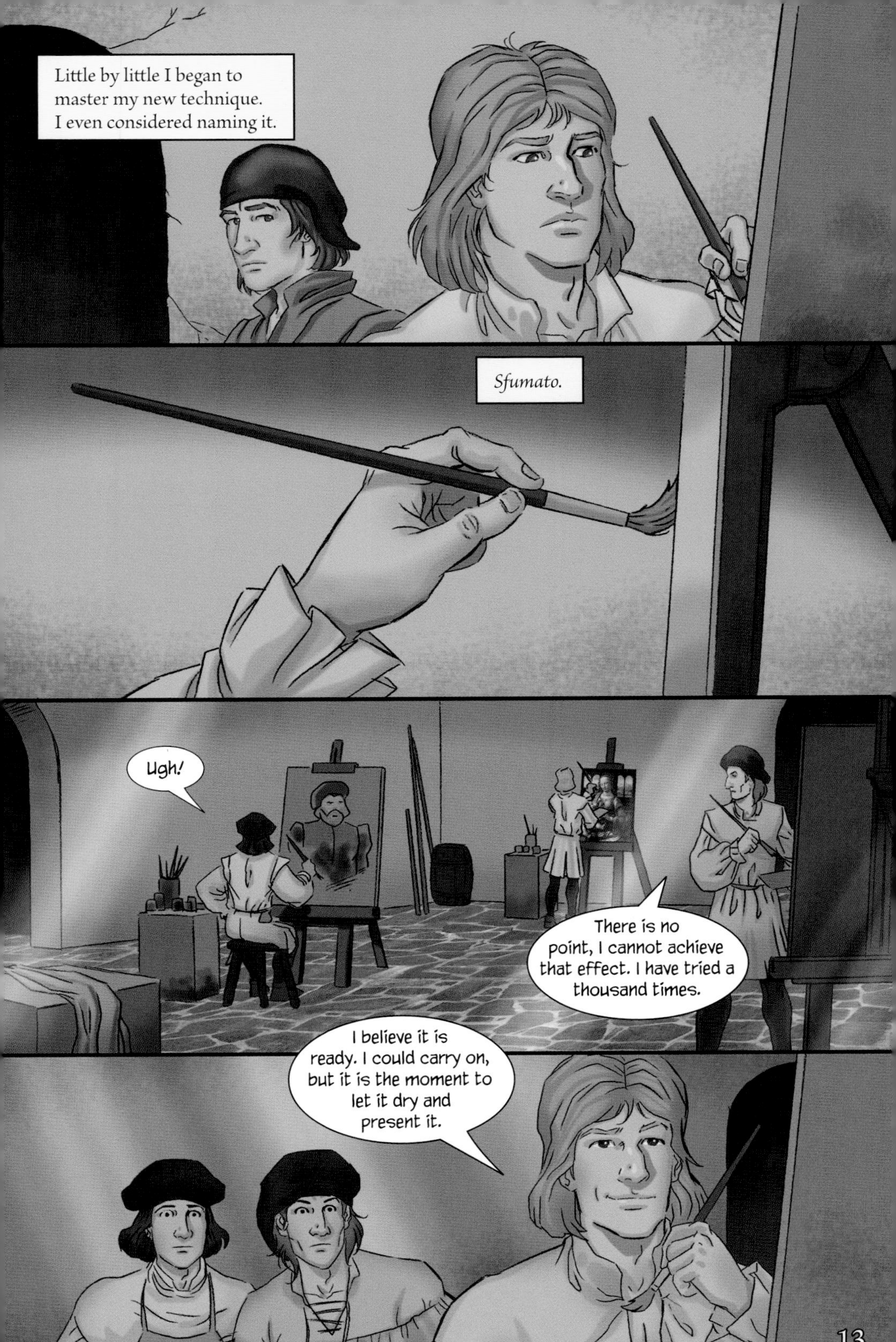

Little by little I began to master my new technique. I even considered naming it.
Sfumato.
Ugh!
There is no point, I cannot achieve that effect. I have tried a thousand times.
I believe it is ready. I could carry on, but it is the moment to let it dry and present it.

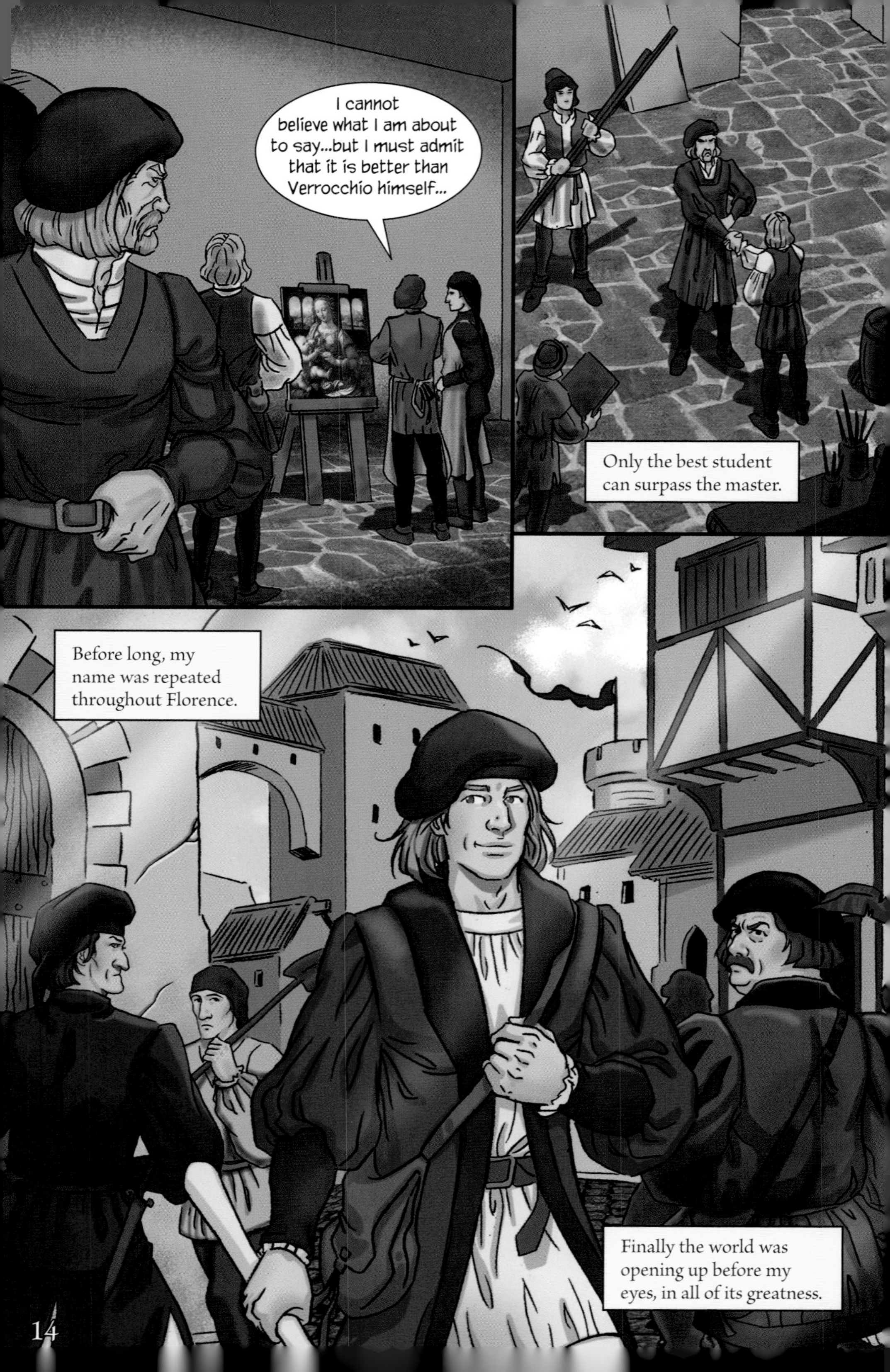
I cannot believe what I am about to say...but I must admit that it is better than Verrocchio himself...
Only the best student can surpass the master.
Before long, my name was repeated throughout Florence.
Finally the world was opening up before my eyes, in all of its greatness.

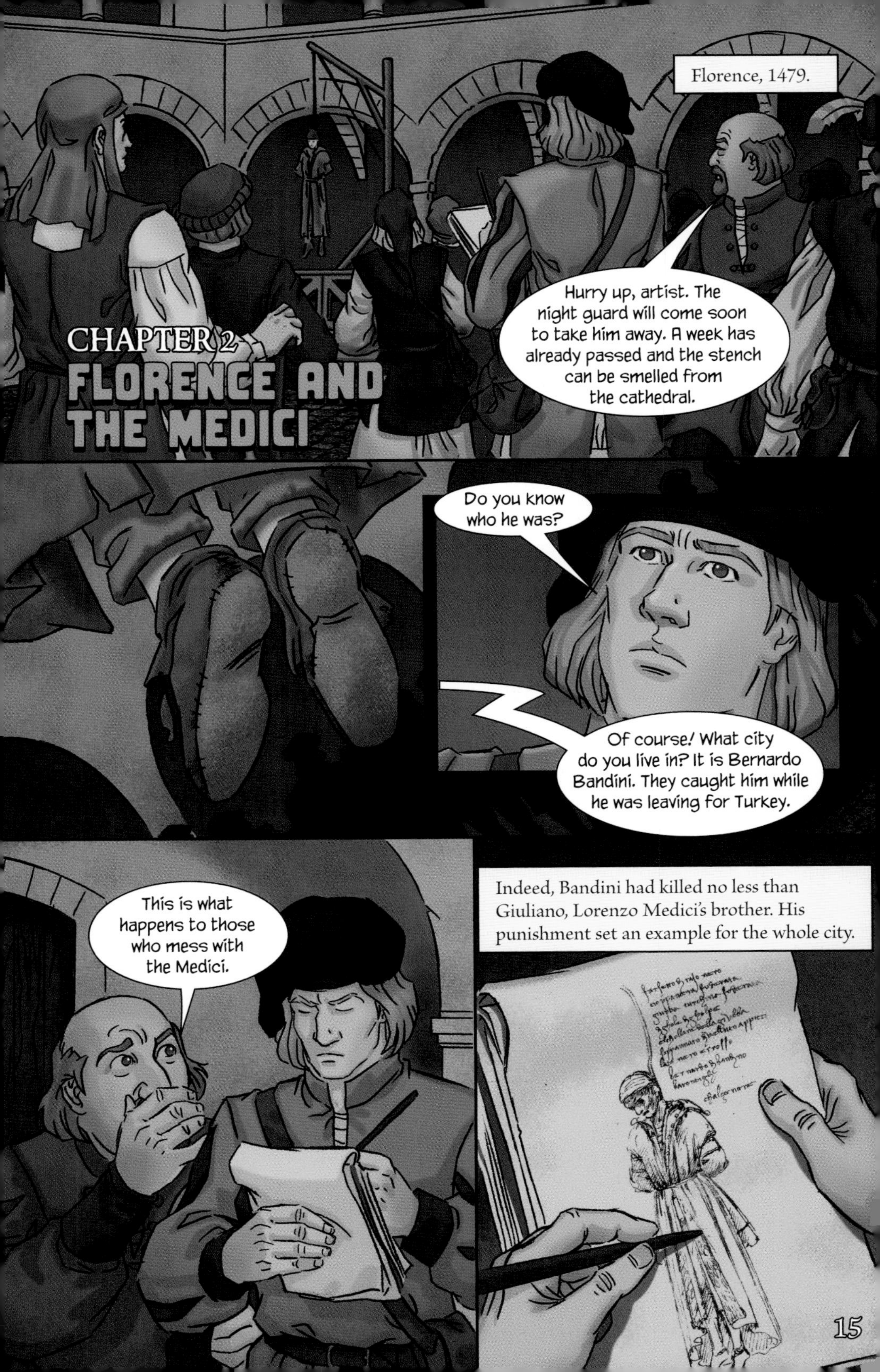
Florence, 1479.
CHAPTER 2
FLORENCE AND THE MEDICI
Hurry up, artist. The night guard will come soon to take him away. A week has already passed and the stench can be smelled from the cathedral.
Do you know who he was?
Of course! What city do you live in? It is Bernardo Bandini. They caught him while he was leaving for Turkey.
This is what happens to those who mess with the Medici.
Indeed, Bandini had killed no less than Giuliano, Lorenzo Medici's brother. His punishment set an example for the whole city.

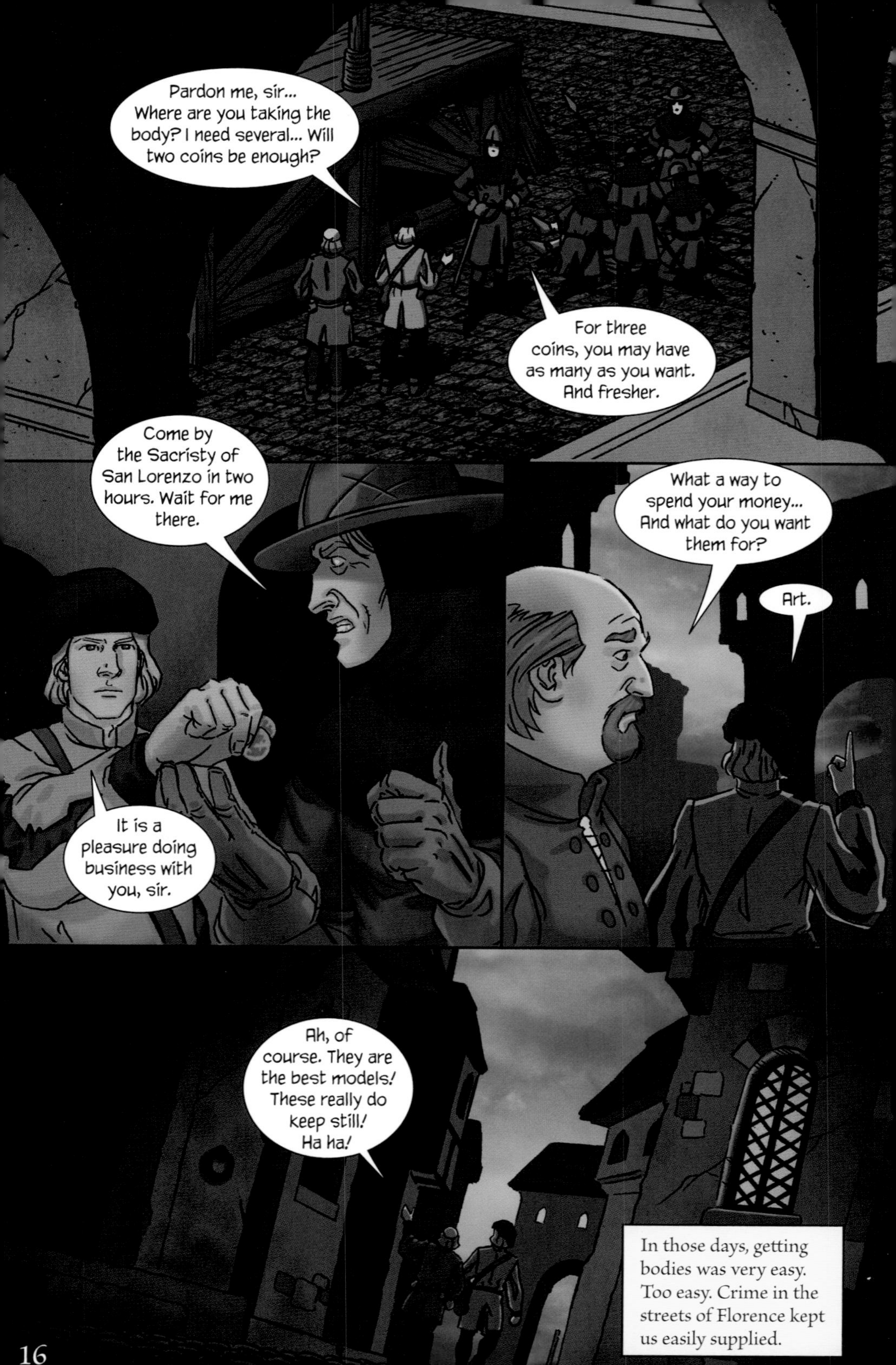
Pardon me, sir... Where are you taking the body? I need several... Will two coins be enough?
For three coins, you may have as many as you want. And fresher.
Come by the Sacristy of San Lorenzo in two hours. Wait for me there.
It is a pleasure doing business with you, sir.
What a way to spend your money... And what do you want them for?
Art.
Ah, of course. They are the best models! These really do keep still! Ha ha!
In those days, getting bodies was very easy. Too easy. Crime in the streets of Florence kept us easily supplied.

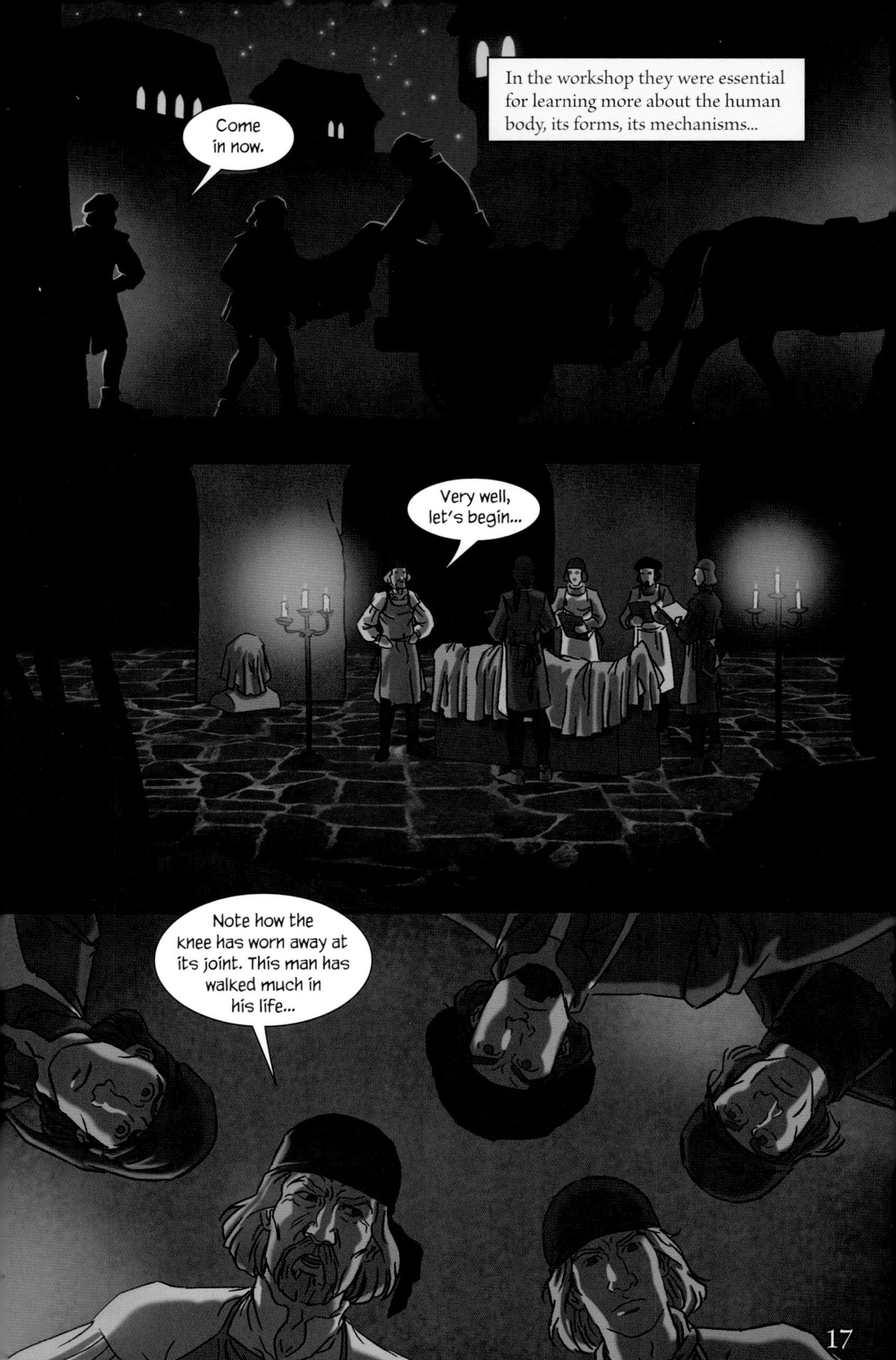

In the workshop they were essential for learning more about the human body, its forms, its mechanisms...
Come in now.
Very well, let's begin...
Note how the knee has worn away at its joint. This man has walked much in his life...

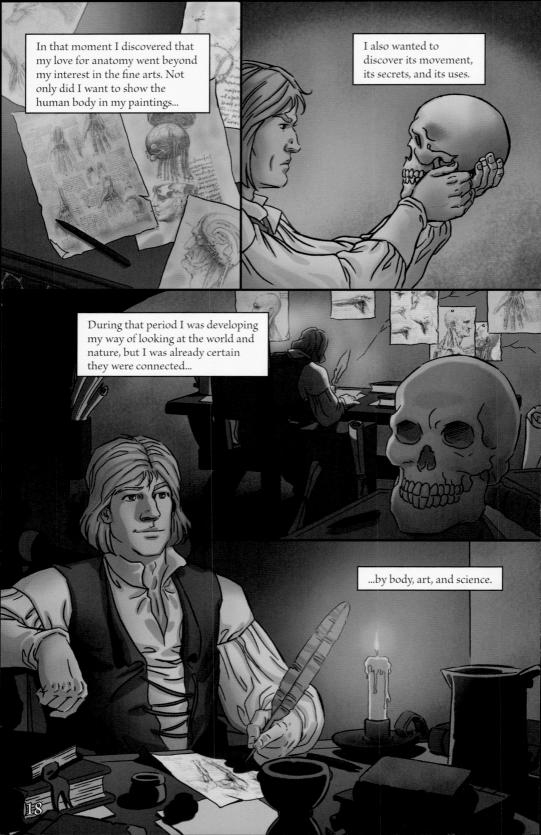

In that moment I discovered that my love for anatomy went beyond my interest in the fine arts. Not only did I want to show the human body in my paintings...

I also wanted to discover its movement, its secrets, and its uses.

During that period I was developing my way of looking at the world and nature, but I was already certain they were connected...

...by body, art, and science.

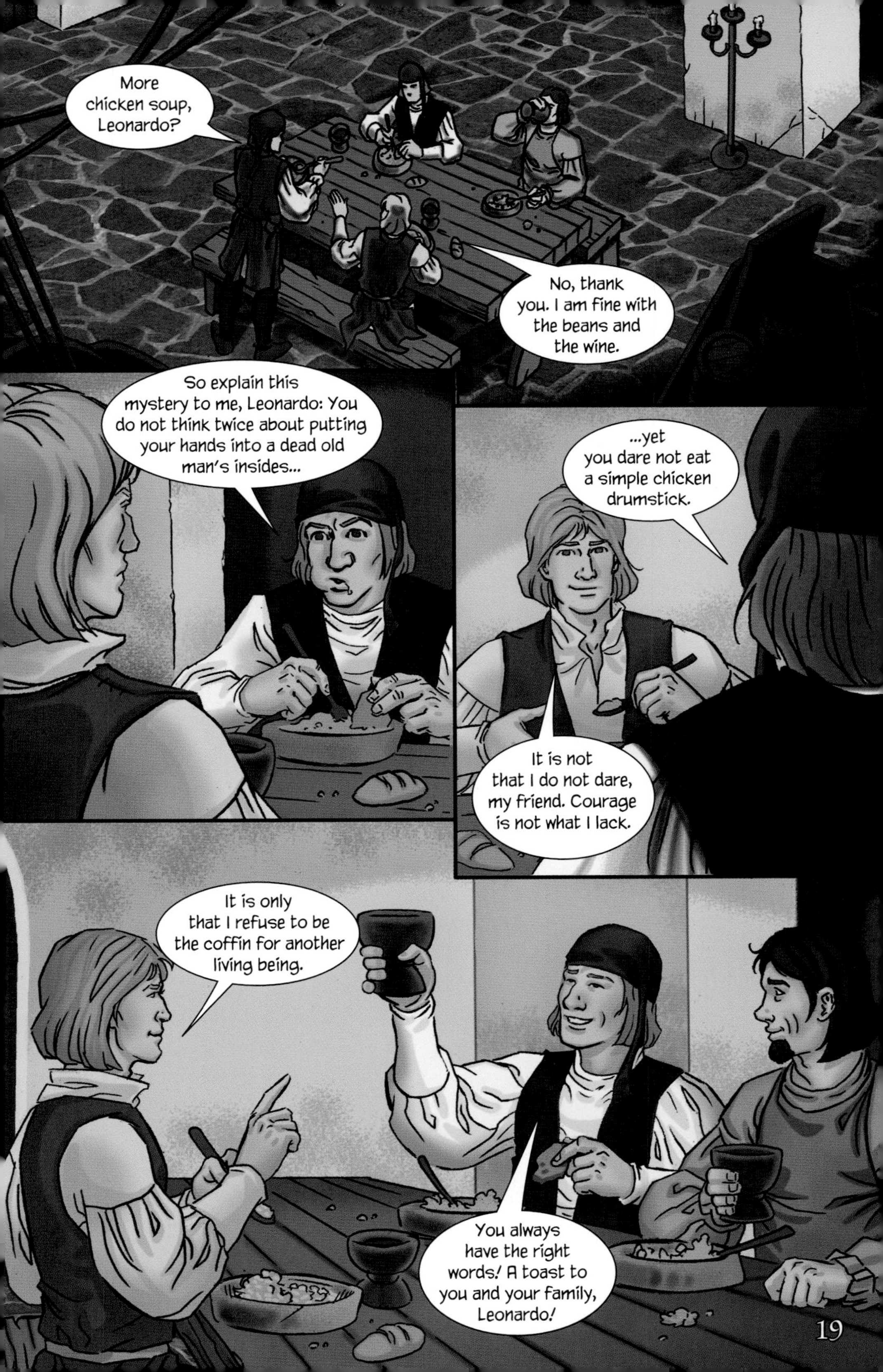
More chicken soup, Leonardo?
No, thank you. I am fine with the beans and the wine.
So explain this mystery to me, Leonardo: You do not think twice about putting your hands into a dead old man's insides...
...yet you dare not eat a simple chicken drumstick.
It is not that I do not dare, my friend. Courage is not what I lack.
It is only that I refuse to be the coffin for another living being.
You always have the right words! A toast to you and your family, Leonardo!

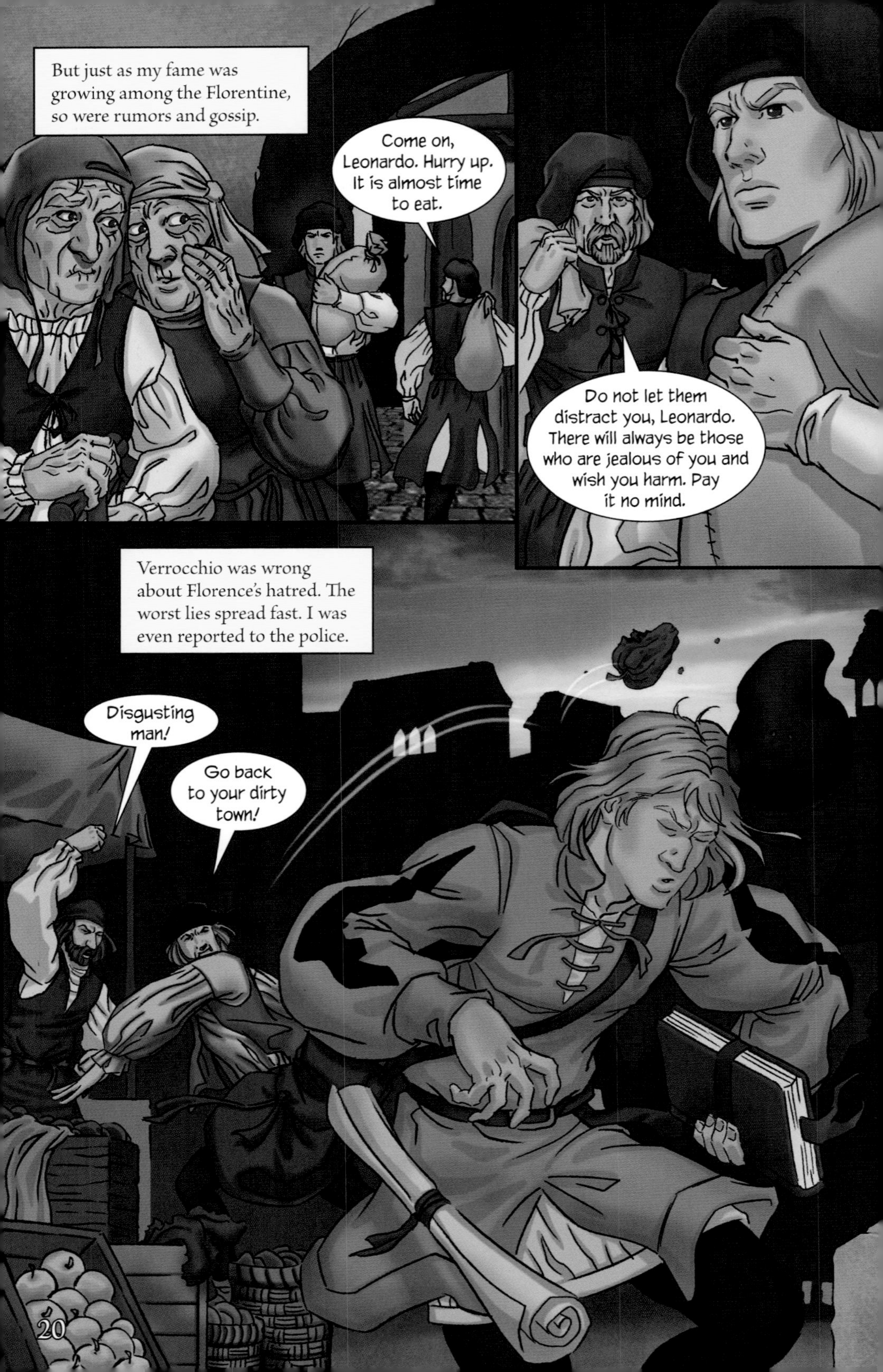
But just as my fame was growing among the Florentine, so were rumors and gossip.
Come on, Leonardo. Hurry up. It is almost time to eat.
Do not let them distract you, Leonardo. There will always be those who are jealous of you and wish you harm. Pay it no mind.
Verrocchio was wrong about Florence's hatred. The worst lies spread fast. I was even reported to the police.
Disgusting man!
Go back to your dirty town!

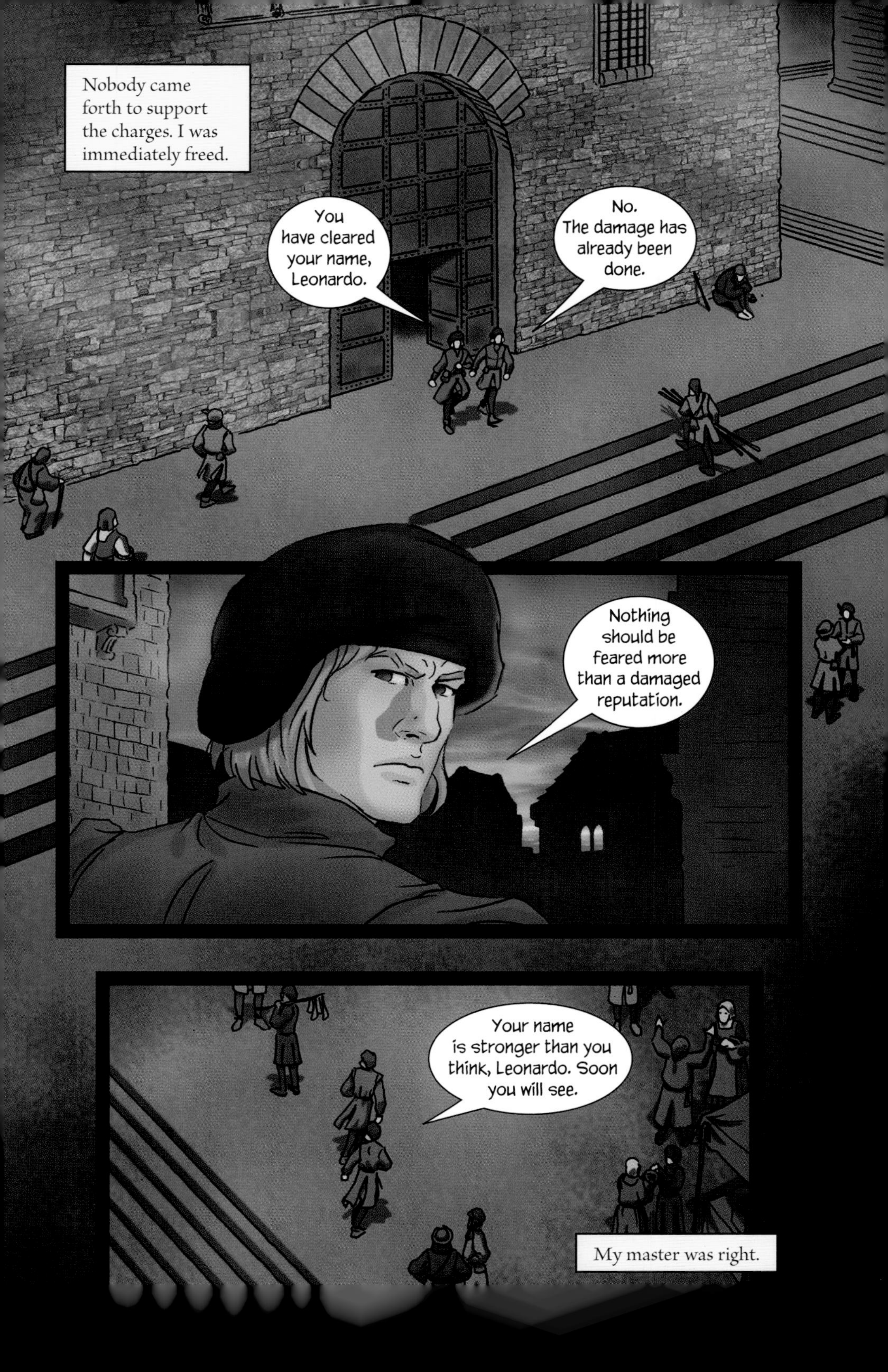
Nobody came forth to support the charges. I was immediately freed.
You have cleared your name, Leonardo.
No. The damage has already been done.
Nothing should be feared more than a damaged reputation.
Your name is stronger than you think, Leonardo. Soon you will see.
My master was right.

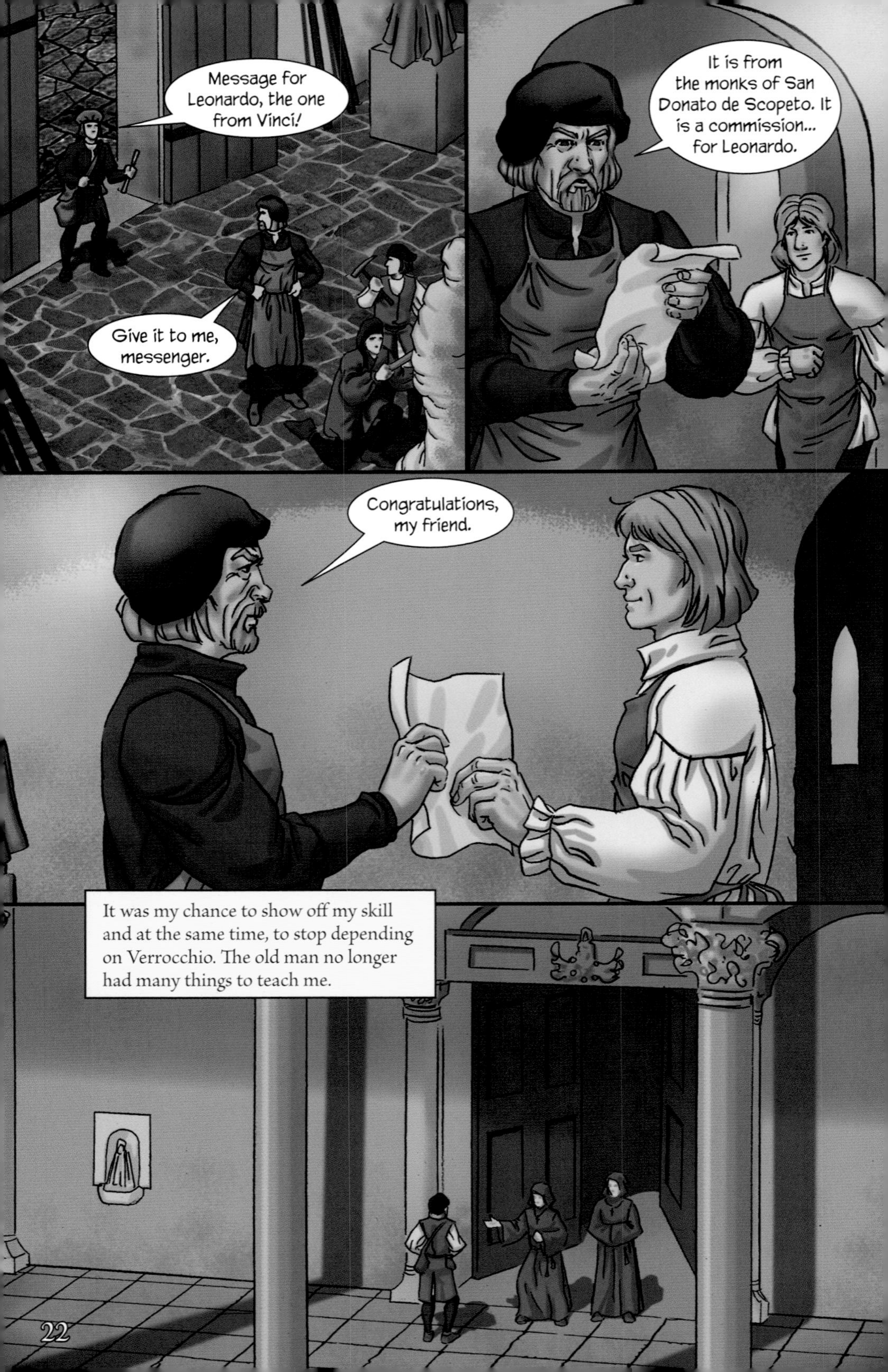

Message for Leonardo, the one from Vinci!
Give it to me, messenger.
It is from the monks of San Donato de Scopeto. It is a commission... for Leonardo.
Congratulations, my friend.
It was my chance to show off my skill and at the same time, to stop depending on Verrocchio. The old man no longer had many things to teach me.

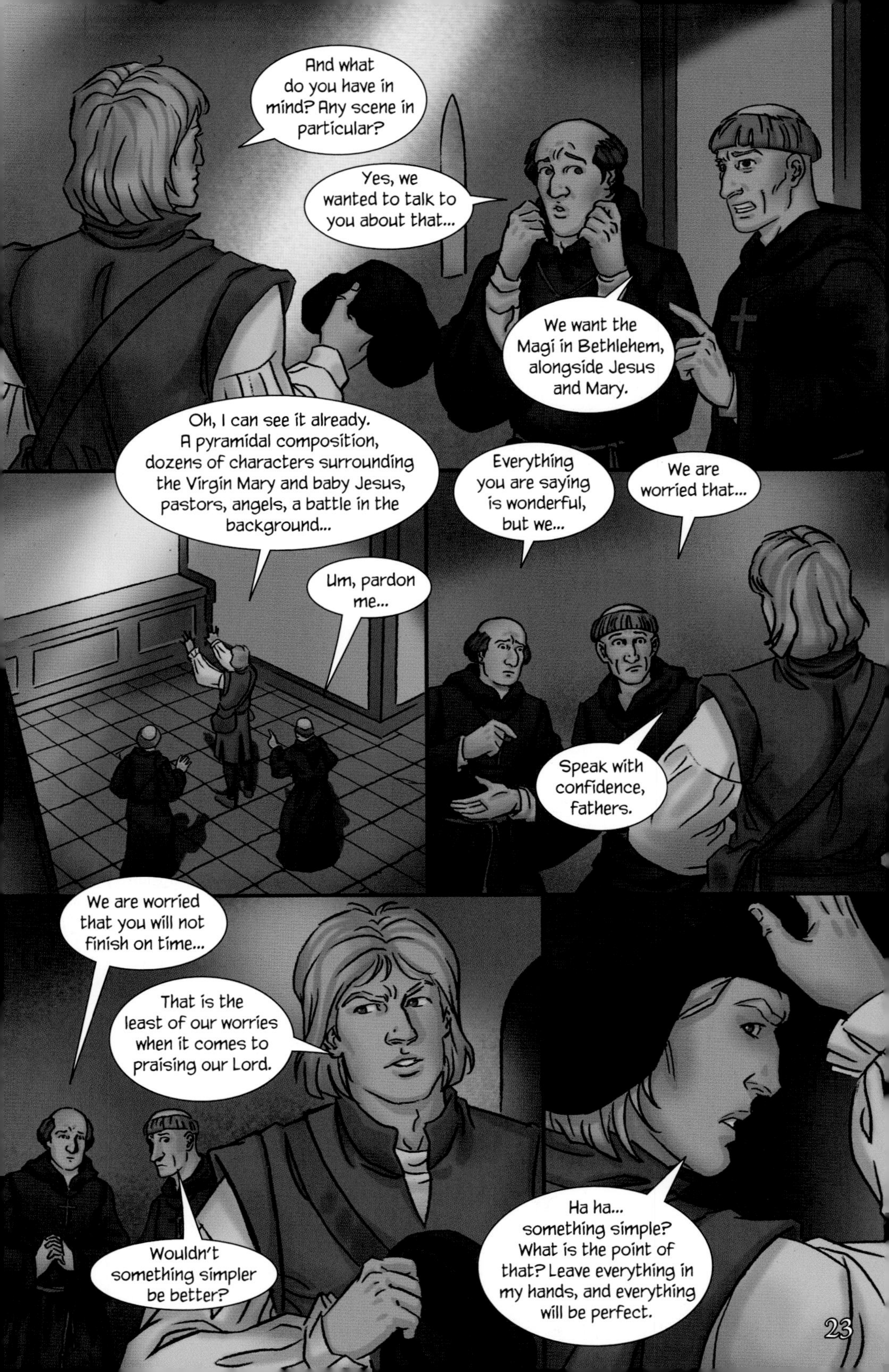
And what do you have in mind? Any scene in particular?
Yes, we wanted to talk to you about that...
We want the Magi in Bethlehem, alongside Jesus and Mary.
Oh, I can see it already. A pyramidal composition, dozens of characters surrounding the Virgin Mary and baby Jesus, pastors, angels, a battle in the background...
Um, pardon me...
Everything you are saying is wonderful, but we...
We are worried that...
Speak with confidence, fathers.
We are worried that you will not finish on time...
That is the least of our worries when it comes to praising our Lord.
Wouldn't something simpler be better?
Ha ha... something simple? What is the point of that? Leave everything in my hands, and everything will be perfect.

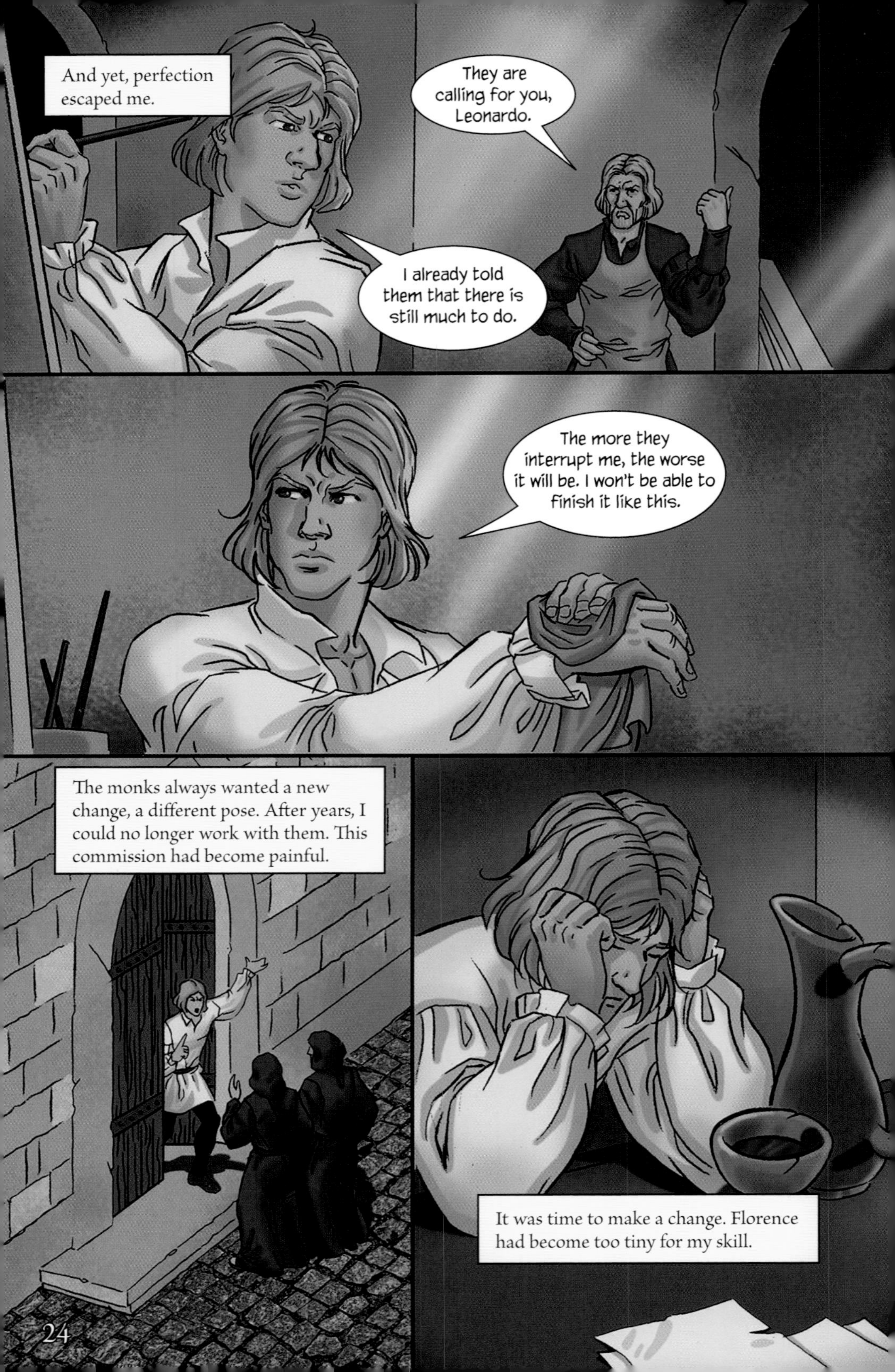
And yet, perfection escaped me.
They are calling for you, Leonardo.
I already told them that there is still much to do.
The more they interrupt me, the worse it will be. I won't be able to finish it like this.
The monks always wanted a new change, a different pose. After years, I could no longer work with them. This commission had become painful.
It was time to make a change. Florence had become too tiny for my skill.

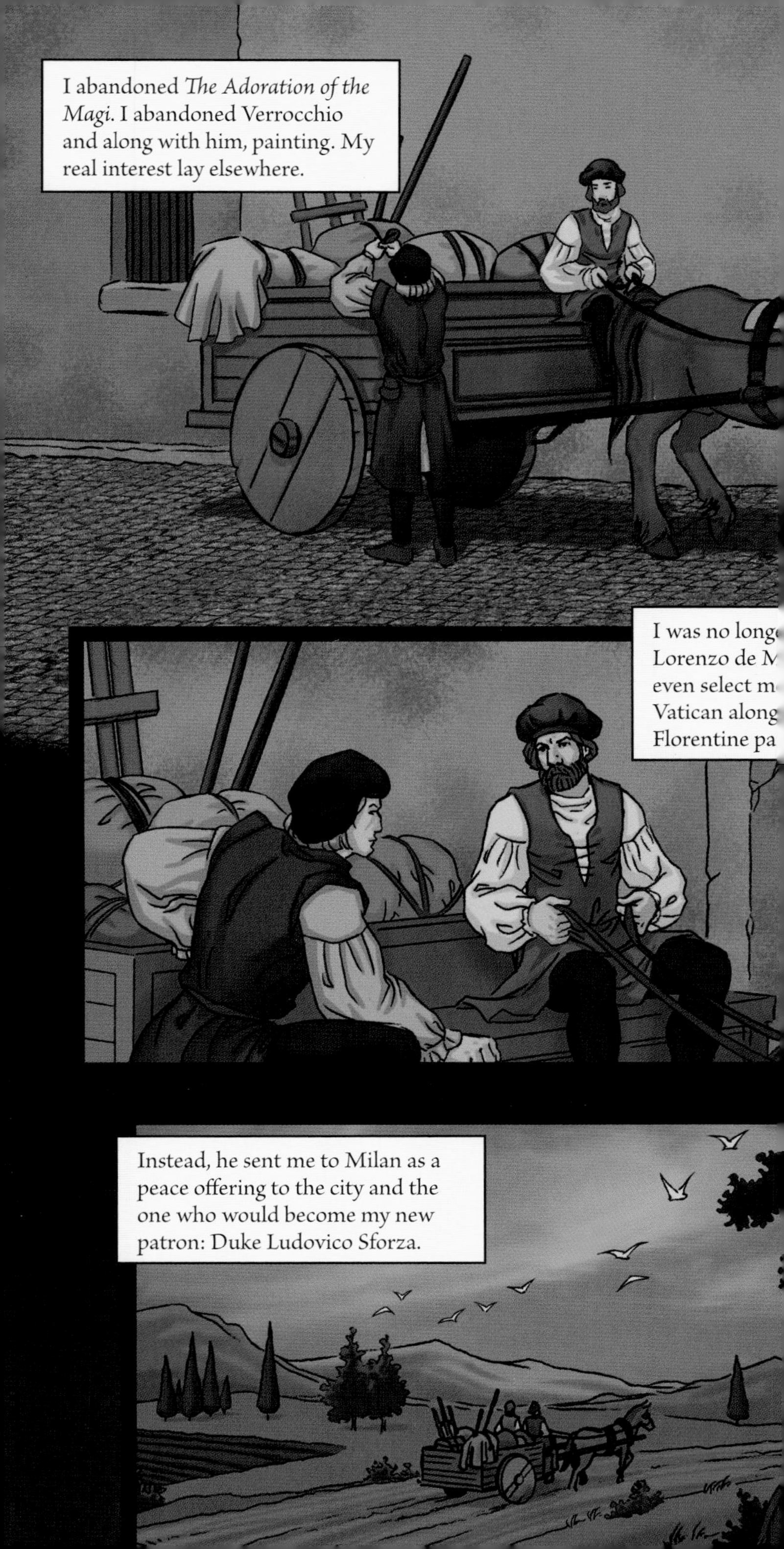
I abandoned *The Adoration of the Magi*. I abandoned Verrocchio and along with him, painting. My real interest lay elsewhere.
I was no long
Lorenzo de M
even select m
Vatican along
Florentine pa
Instead, he sent me to Milan as a peace offering to the city and the one who would become my new patron: Duke Ludovico Sforza.

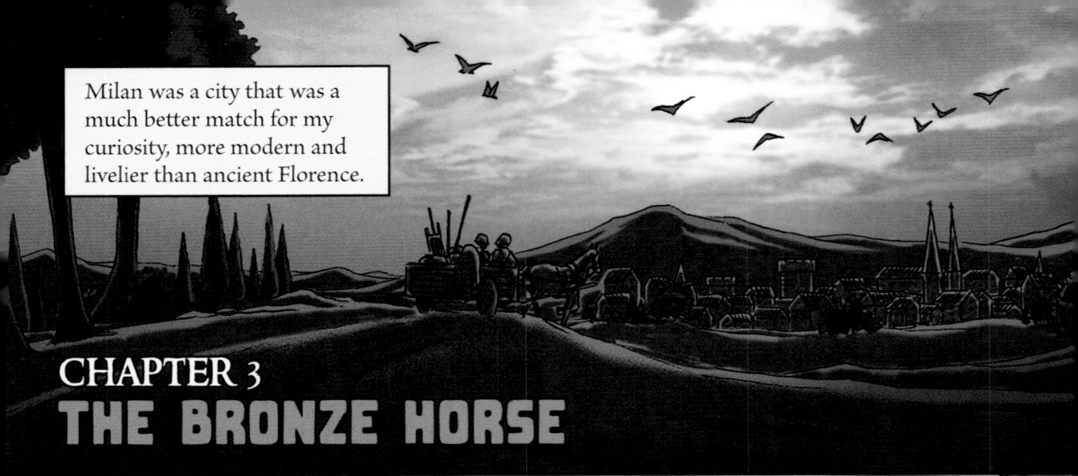
Milan was a city that was a much better match for my curiosity, more modern and livelier than ancient Florence.

CHAPTER 3
THE BRONZE HORSE

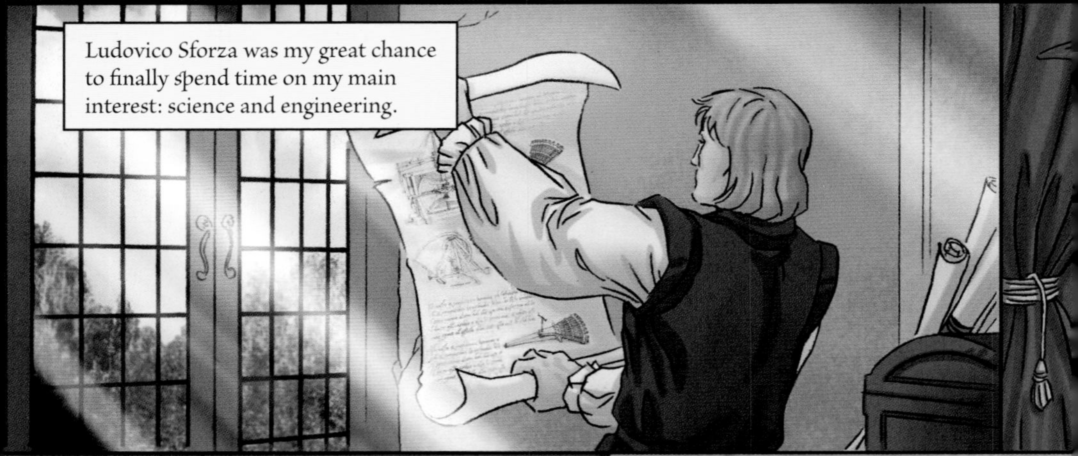
Ludovico Sforza was my great chance to finally spend time on my main interest: science and engineering.

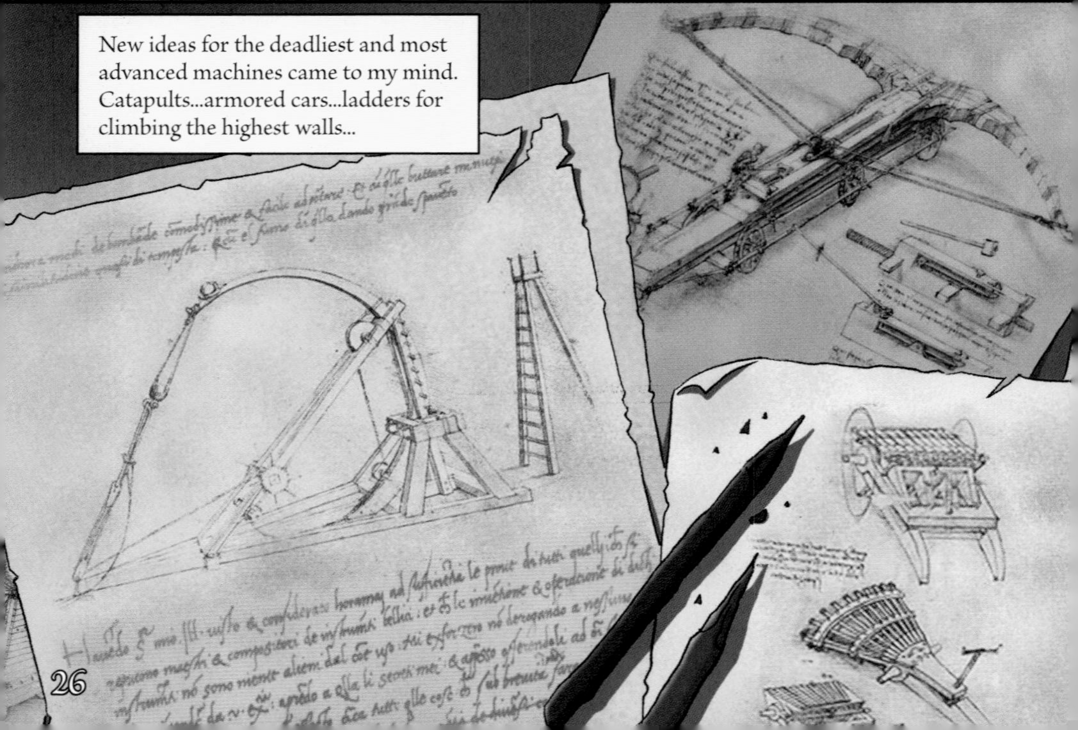
New ideas for the deadliest and most advanced machines came to my mind. Catapults...armored cars...ladders for climbing the highest walls...

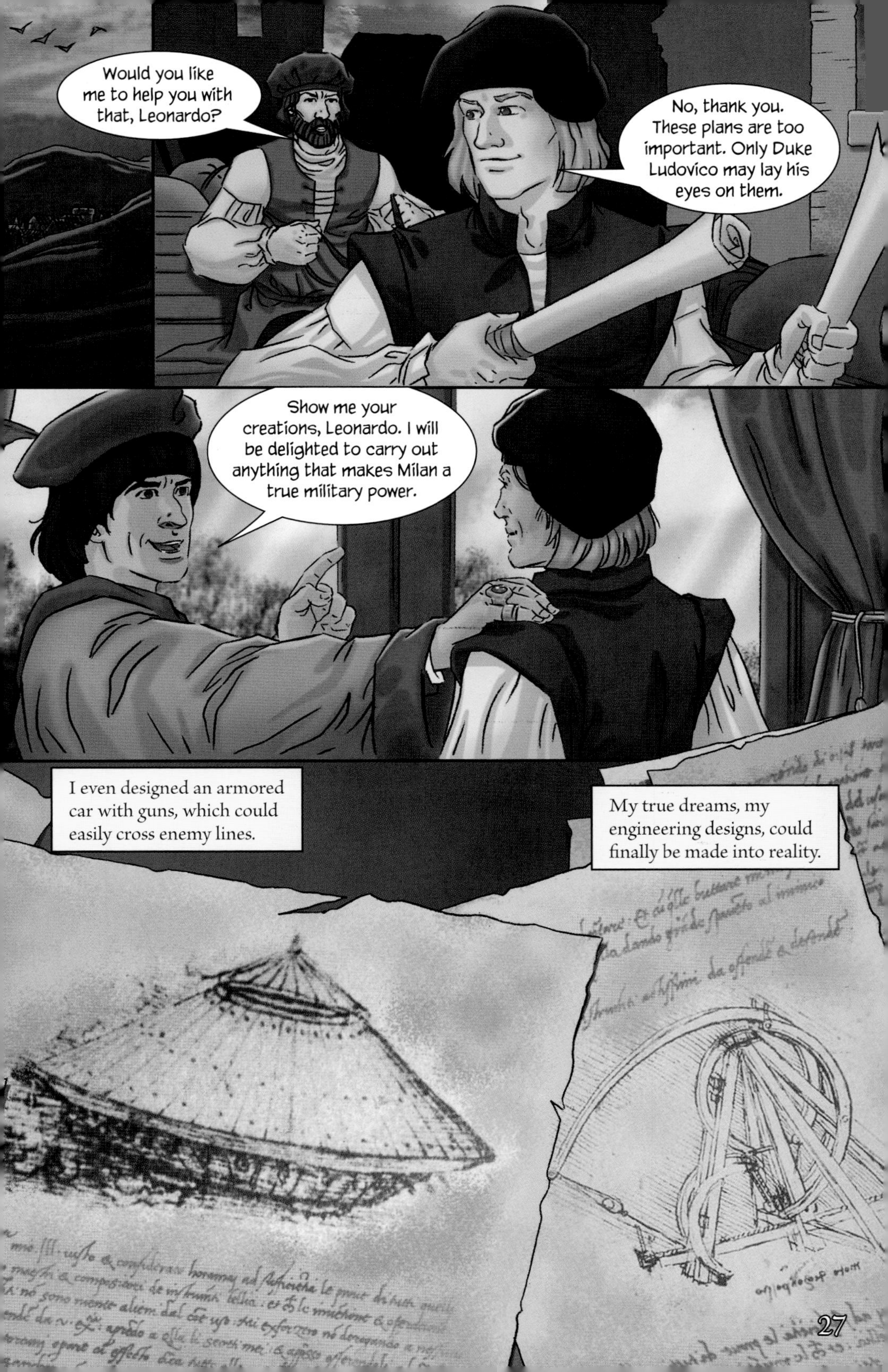
Would you like me to help you with that, Leonardo?
No, thank you. These plans are too important. Only Duke Ludovico may lay his eyes on them.
Show me your creations, Leonardo. I will be delighted to carry out anything that makes Milan a true military power.
I even designed an armored car with guns, which could easily cross enemy lines.
My true dreams, my engineering designs, could finally be made into reality.

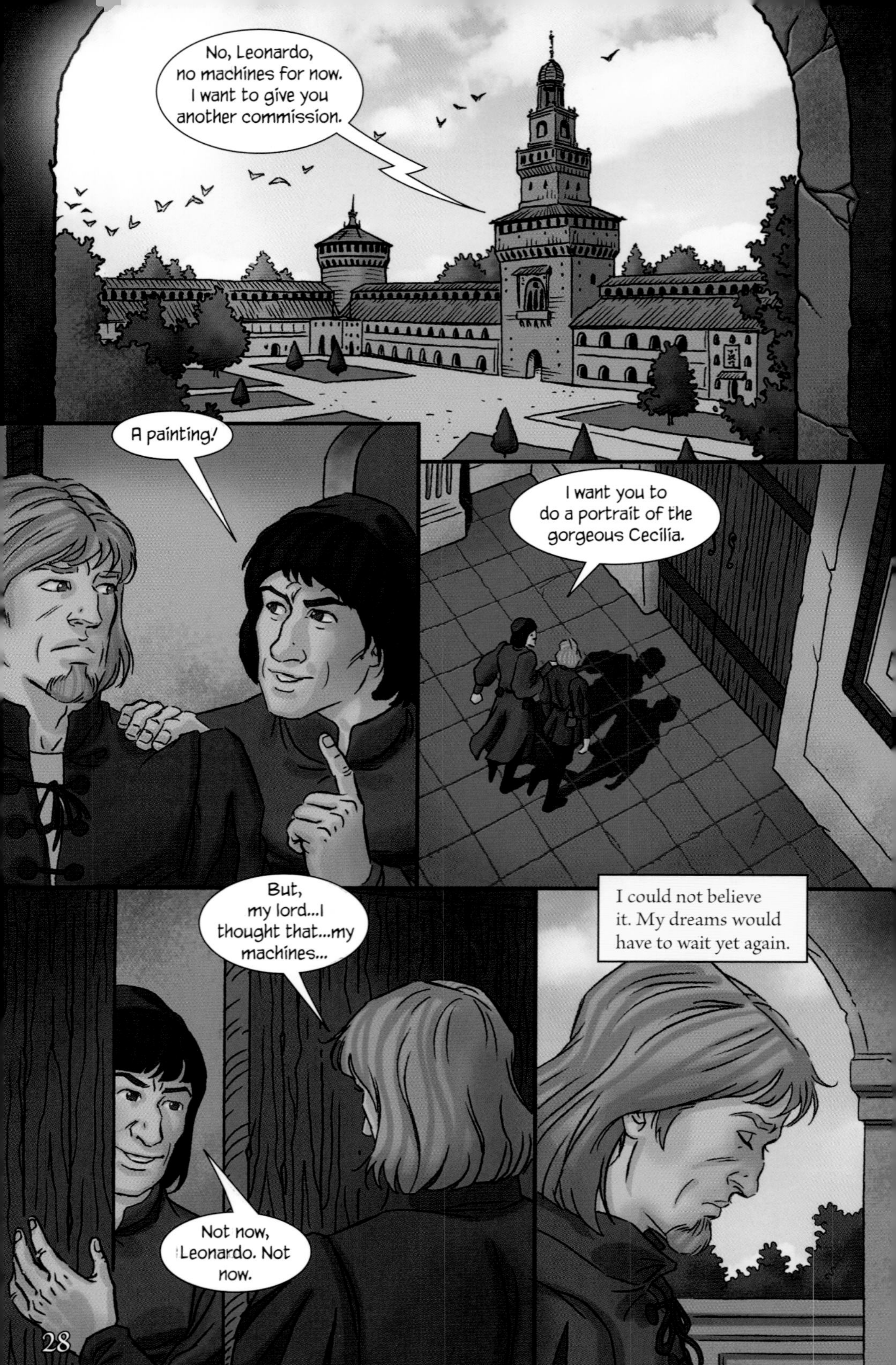
No, Leonardo, no machines for now. I want to give you another commission.
A painting!
I want you to do a portrait of the gorgeous Cecilia.
But, my lord...I thought that...my machines...
Not now, Leonardo. Not now.
I could not believe it. My dreams would have to wait yet again.

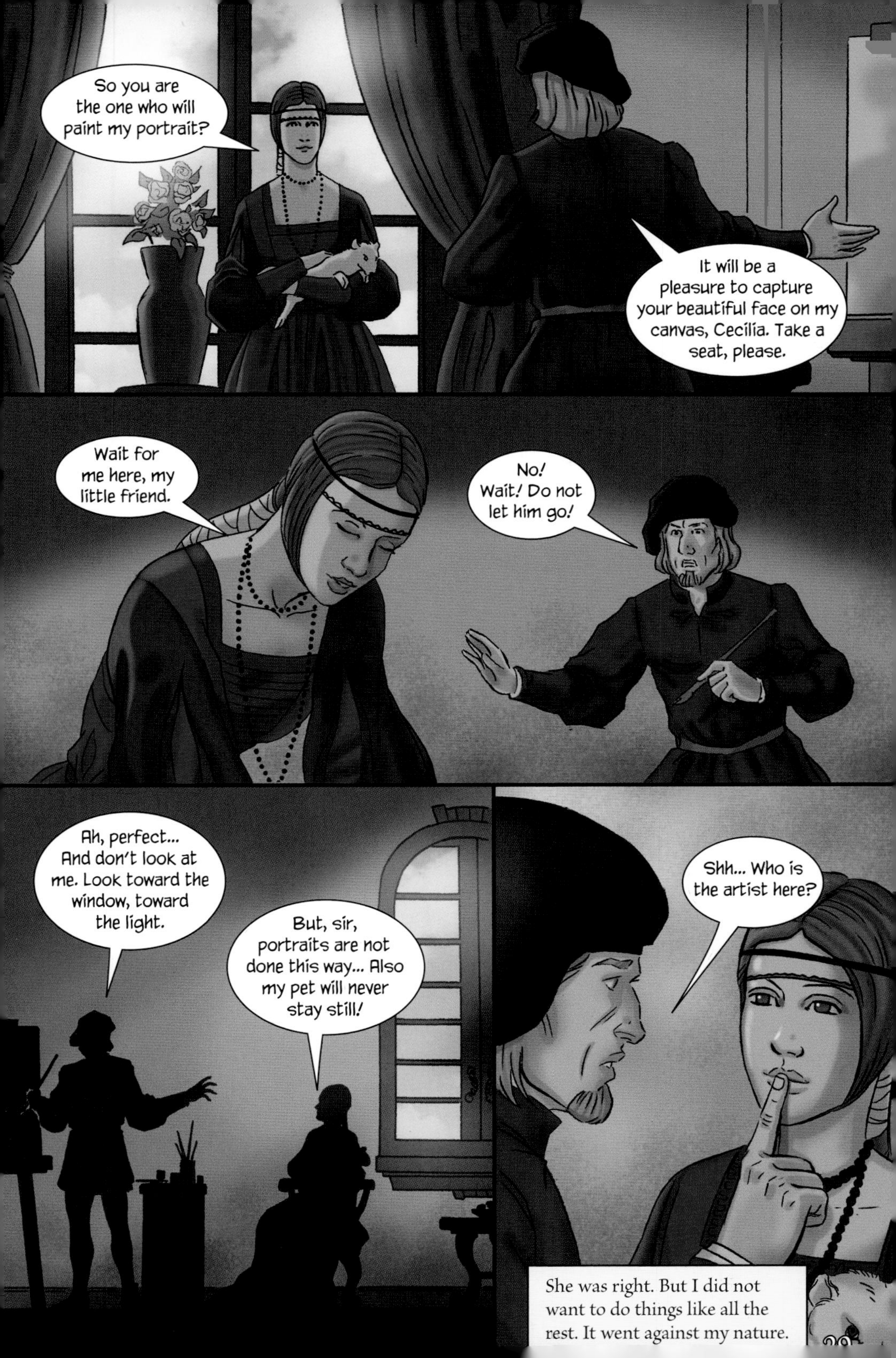
So you are the one who will paint my portrait?
It will be a pleasure to capture your beautiful face on my canvas, Cecilia. Take a seat, please.
Wait for me here, my little friend.
No! Wait! Do not let him go!
Ah, perfect... And don't look at me. Look toward the window, toward the light.
But, sir, portraits are not done this way... Also my pet will never stay still!
Shh... Who is the artist here?
She was right. But I did not want to do things like all the rest. It went against my nature.

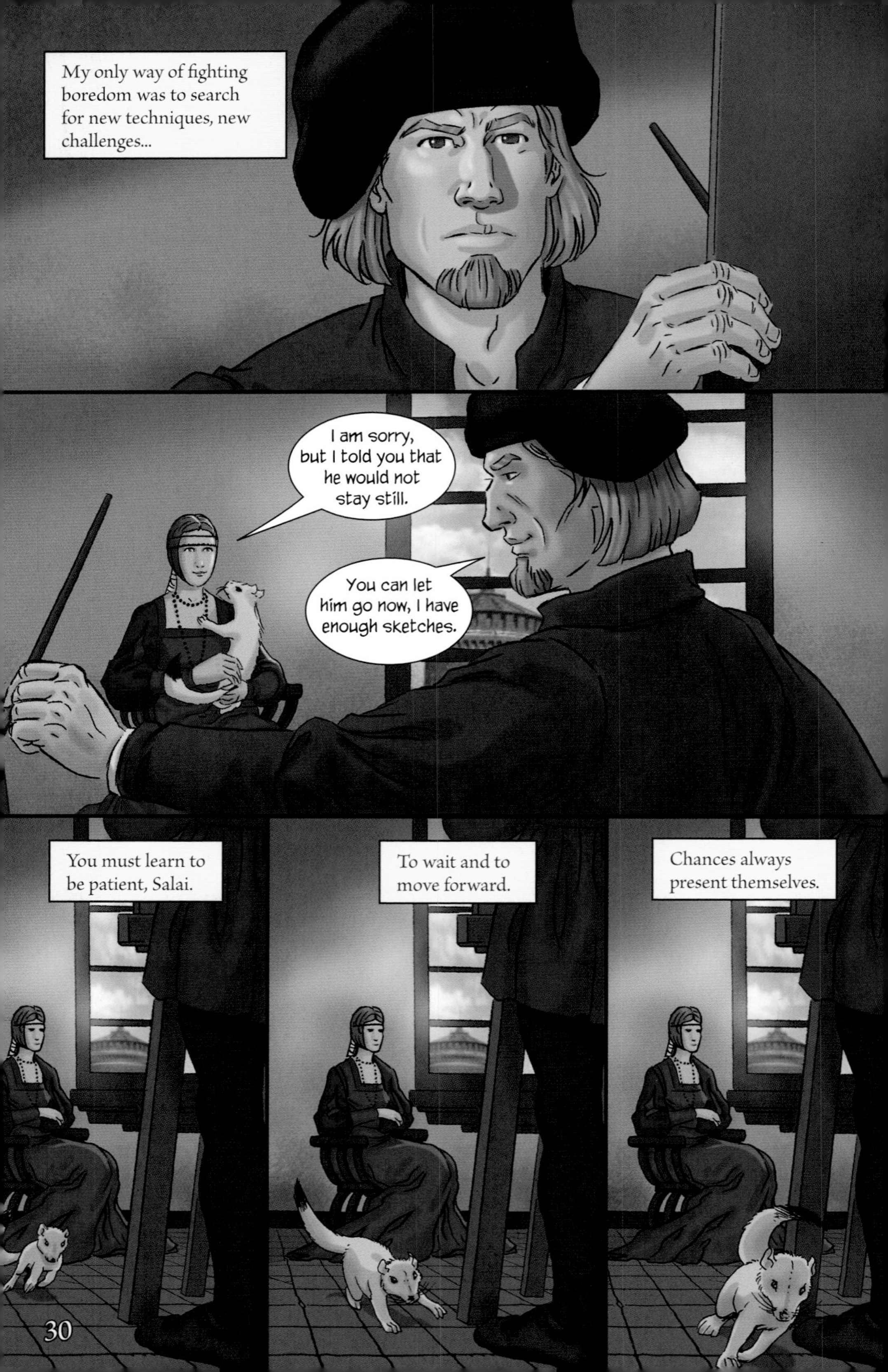
My only way of fighting boredom was to search for new techniques, new challenges...
I am sorry, but I told you that he would not stay still.
You can let him go now, I have enough sketches.
You must learn to be patient, Salai.
To wait and to move forward.
Chances always present themselves.

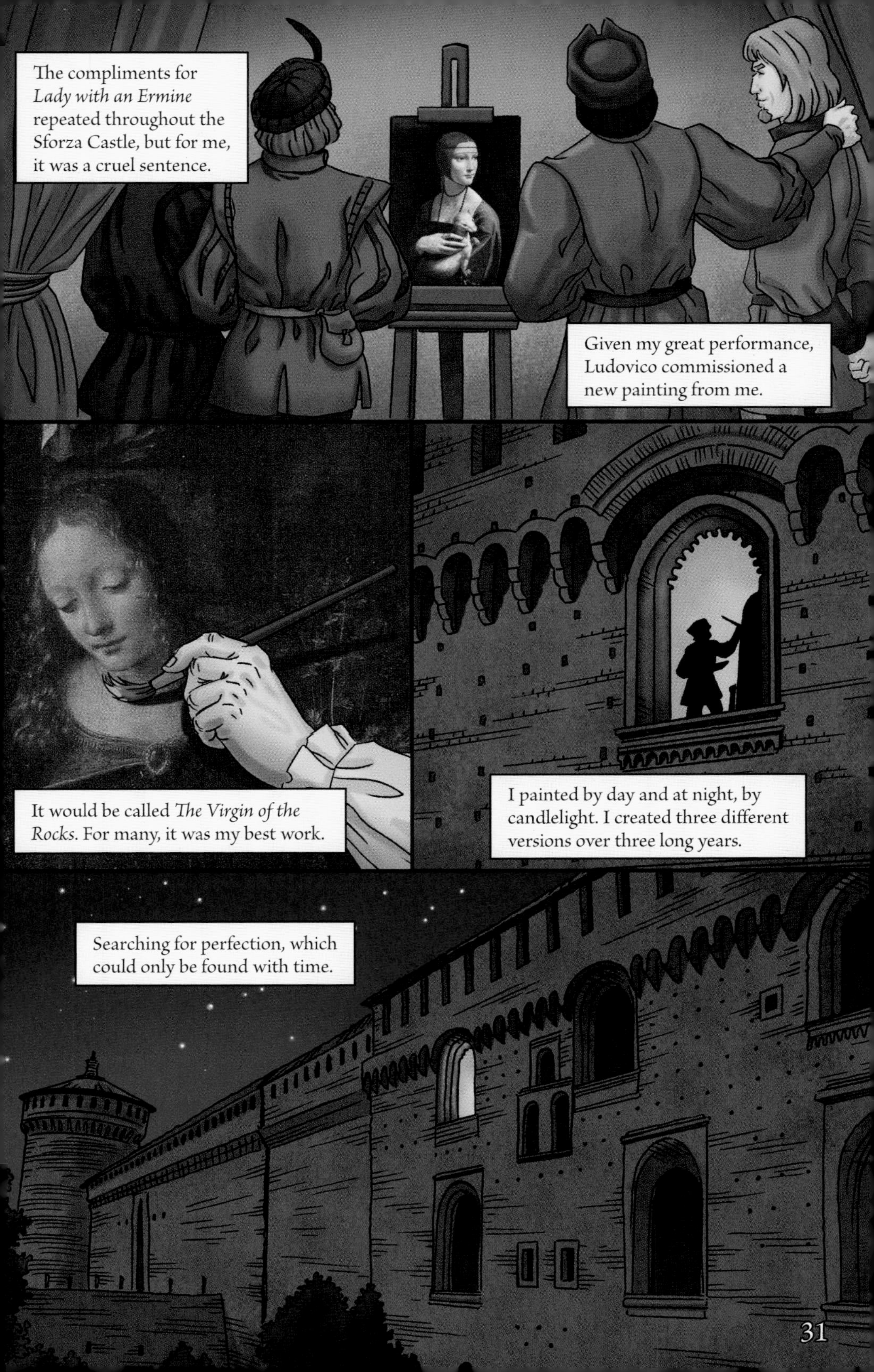

The compliments for *Lady with an Ermine* repeated throughout the Sforza Castle, but for me, it was a cruel sentence.
Given my great performance, Ludovico commissioned a new painting from me.
It would be called *The Virgin of the Rocks*. For many, it was my best work.
I painted by day and at night, by candlelight. I created three different versions over three long years.
Searching for perfection, which could only be found with time.

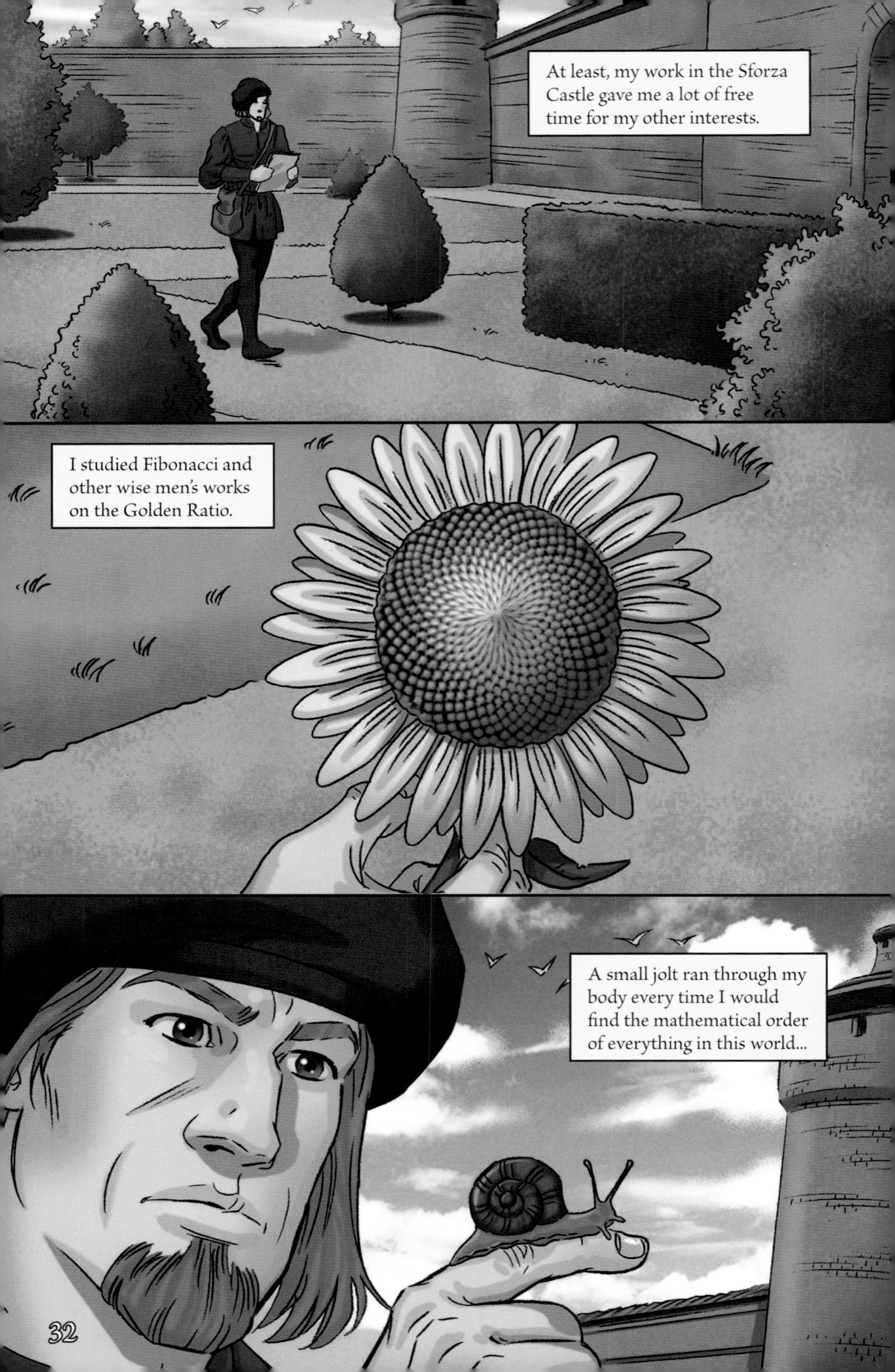
At least, my work in the Sforza Castle gave me a lot of free time for my other interests.
I studied Fibonacci and other wise men's works on the Golden Ratio.
A small jolt ran through my body every time I would find the mathematical order of everything in this world...

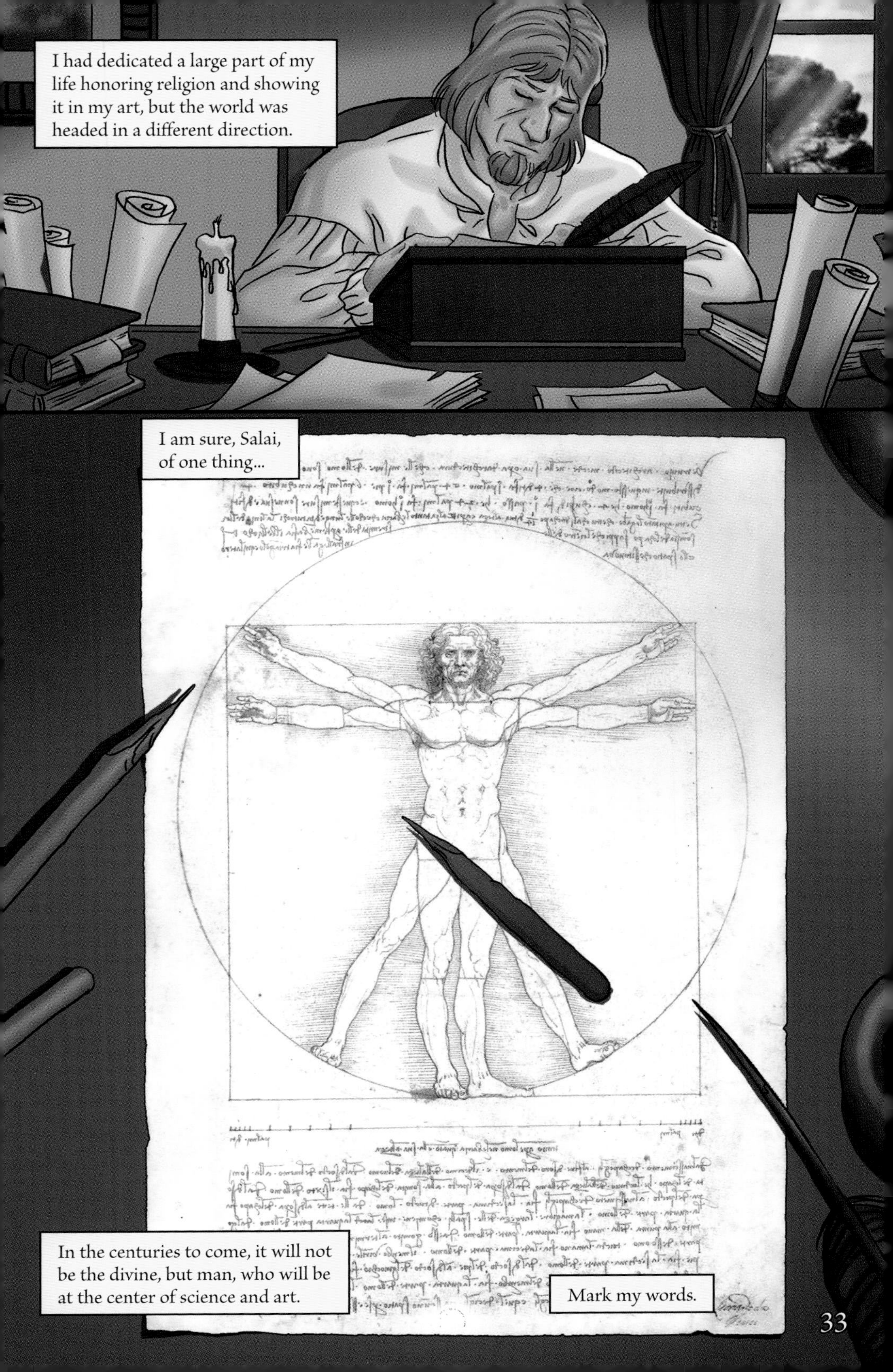

I had dedicated a large part of my life honoring religion and showing it in my art, but the world was headed in a different direction.
I am sure, Salai, of one thing...
In the centuries to come, it will not be the divine, but man, who will be at the center of science and art.
Mark my words.

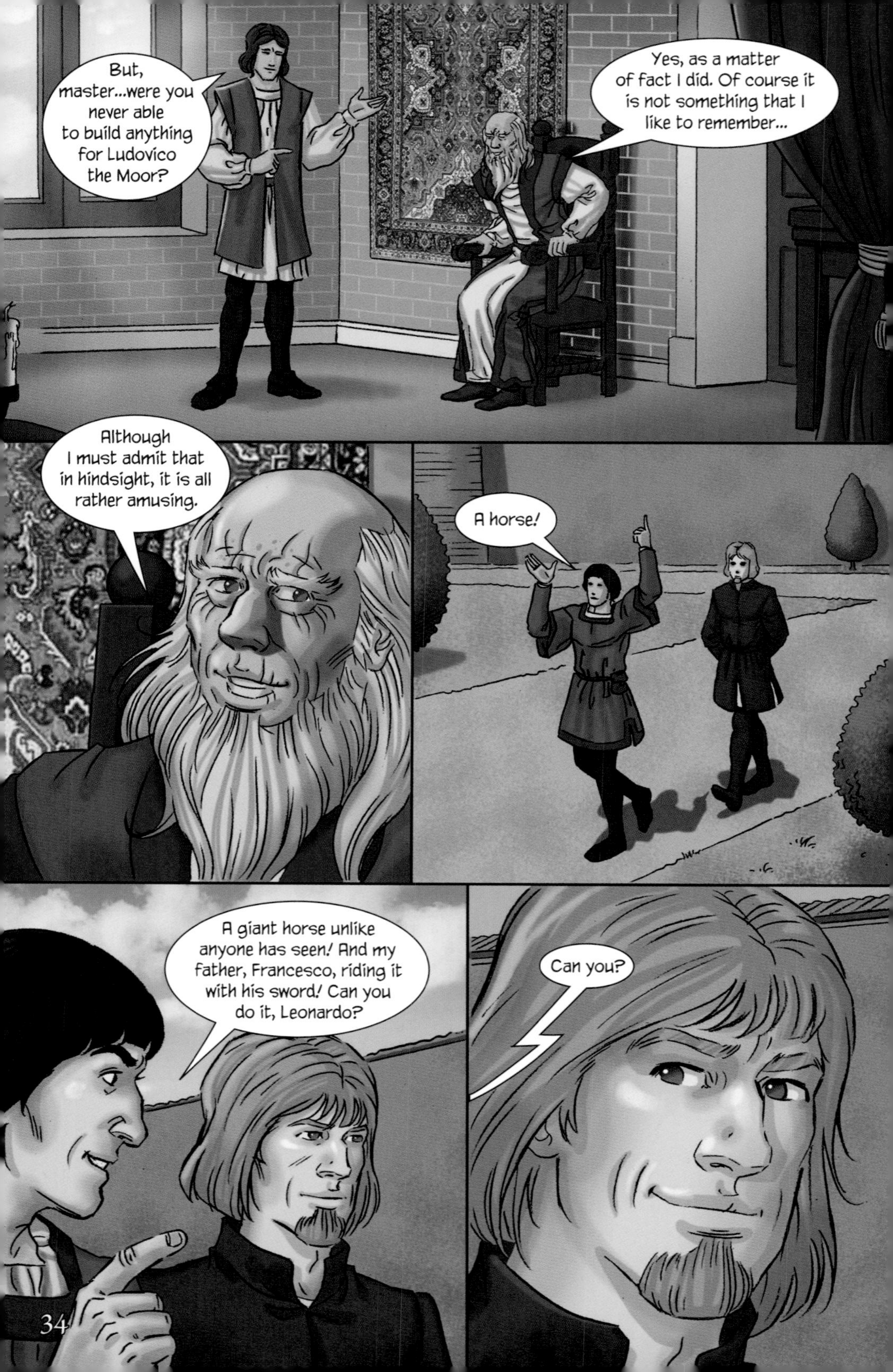
But, master...were you never able to build anything for Ludovico the Moor?
Yes, as a matter of fact I did. Of course it is not something that I like to remember...
Although I must admit that in hindsight, it is all rather amusing.
A horse!
A giant horse unlike anyone has seen! And my father, Francesco, riding it with his sword! Can you do it, Leonardo?
Can you?

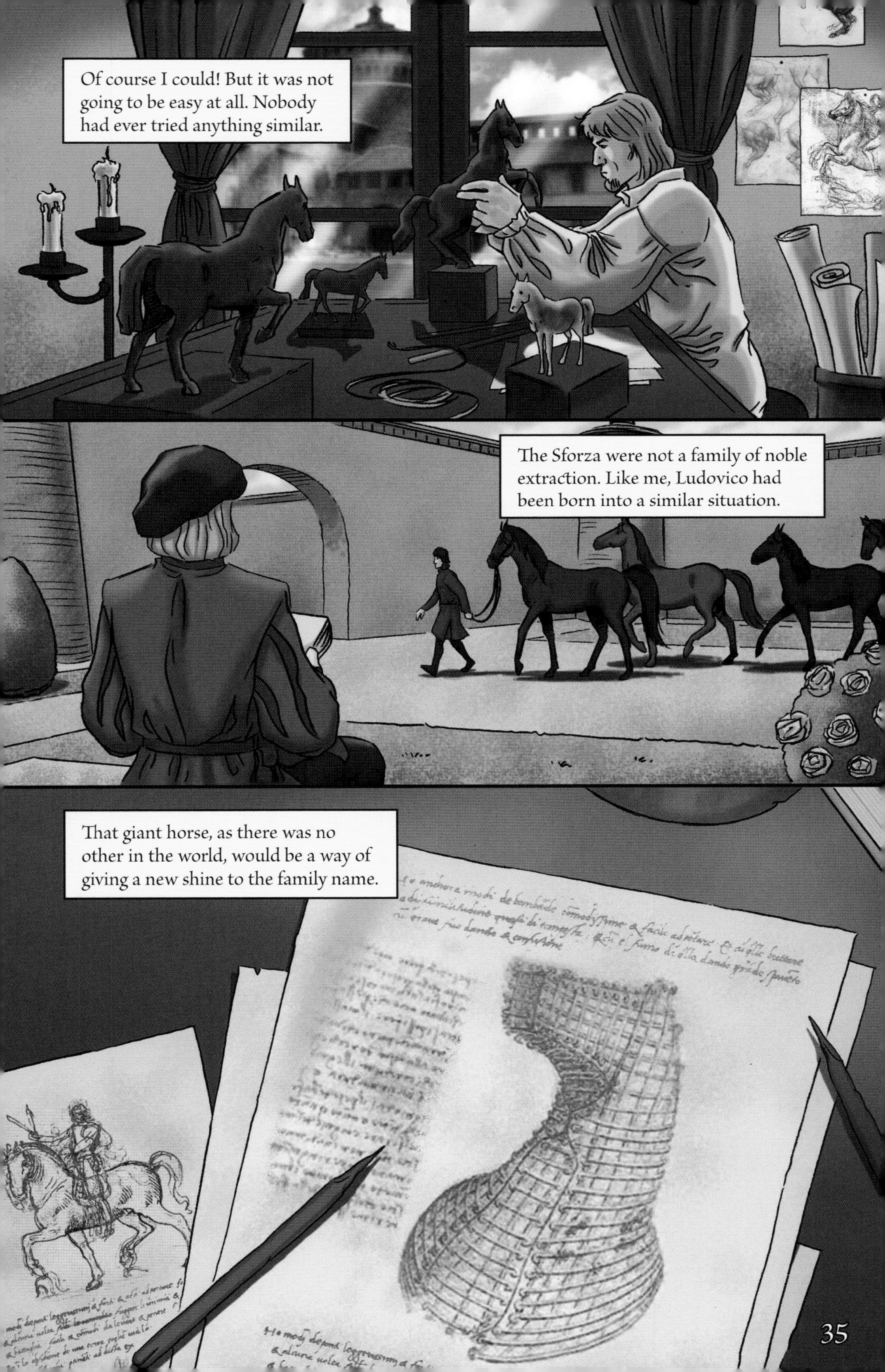

Of course I could! But it was not going to be easy at all. Nobody had ever tried anything similar.
The Sforza were not a family of noble extraction. Like me, Ludovico had been born into a similar situation.
That giant horse, as there was no other in the world, would be a way of giving a new shine to the family name.

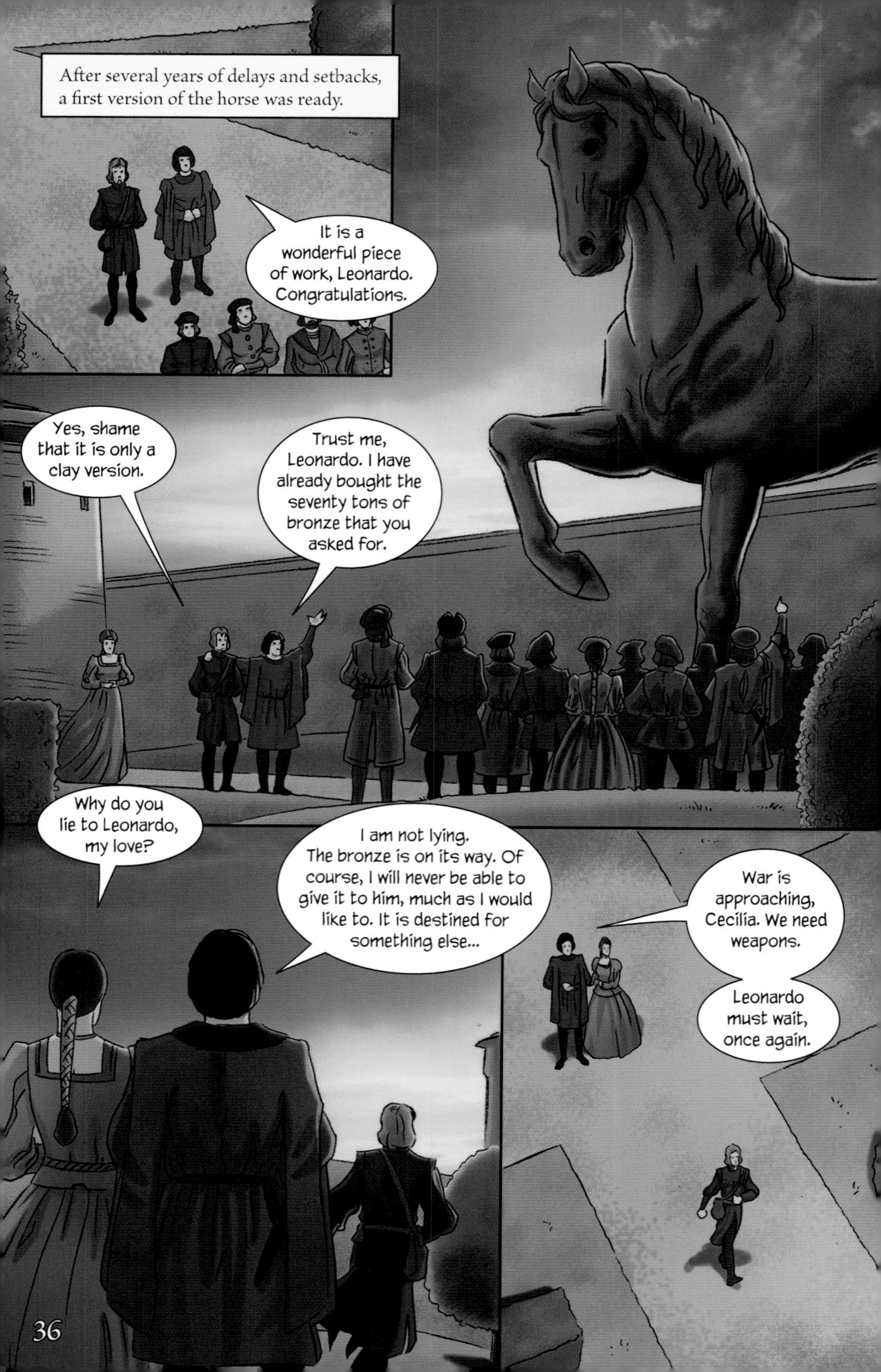
After several years of delays and setbacks, a first version of the horse was ready.
It is a wonderful piece of work, Leonardo. Congratulations.
Yes, shame that it is only a clay version.
Trust me, Leonardo. I have already bought the seventy tons of bronze that you asked for.
Why do you lie to Leonardo, my love?
I am not lying. The bronze is on its way. Of course, I will never be able to give it to him, much as I would like to. It is destined for something else...
War is approaching, Cecilia. We need weapons.
Leonardo must wait, once again.

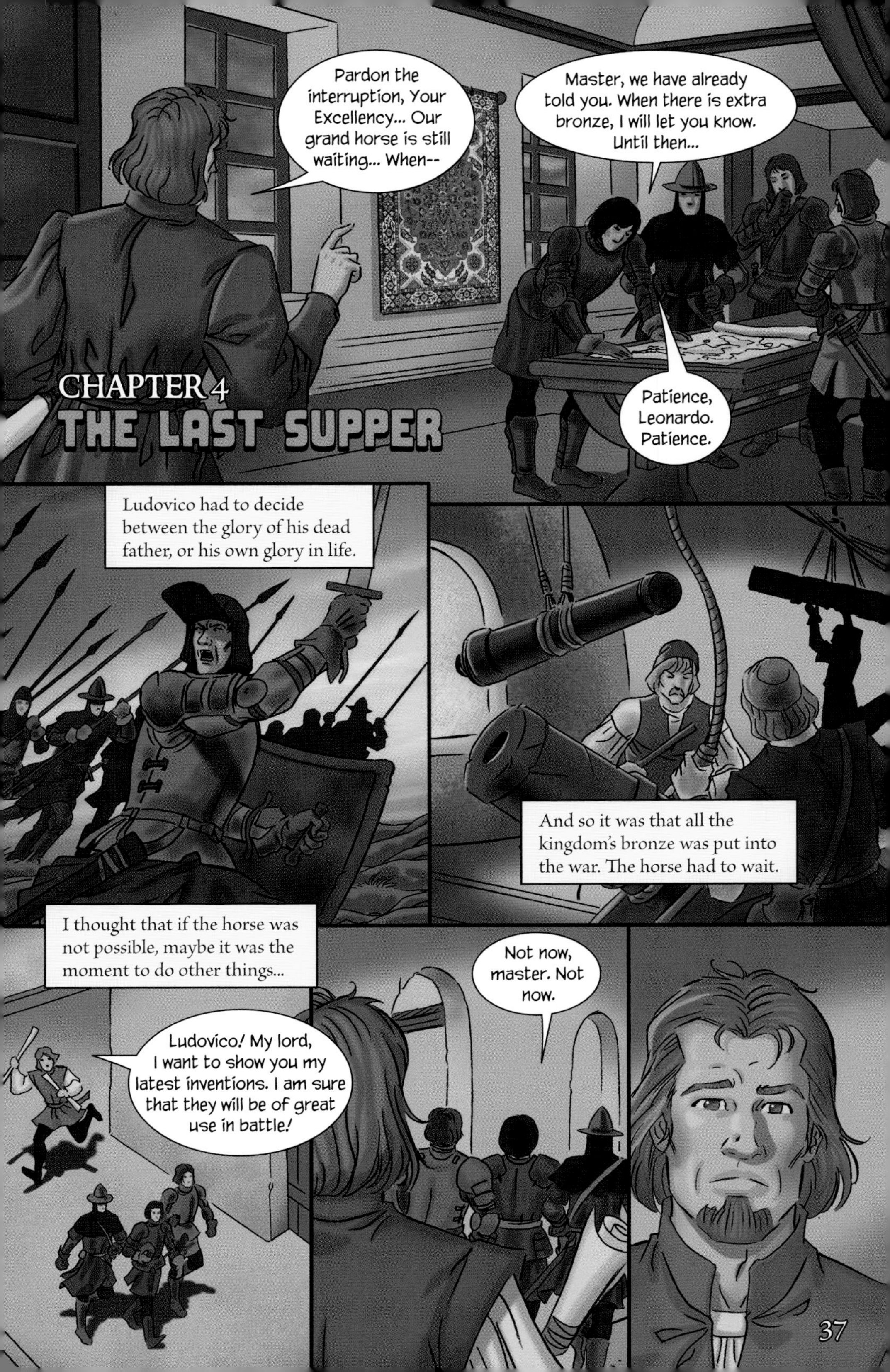
Pardon the interruption, Your Excellency... Our grand horse is still waiting... When--
Master, we have already told you. When there is extra bronze, I will let you know. Until then...
Patience, Leonardo. Patience.
CHAPTER 4
THE LAST SUPPER
Ludovico had to decide between the glory of his dead father, or his own glory in life.
And so it was that all the kingdom's bronze was put into the war. The horse had to wait.
I thought that if the horse was not possible, maybe it was the moment to do other things...
Ludovico! My lord, I want to show you my latest inventions. I am sure that they will be of great use in battle!
Not now, master. Not now.

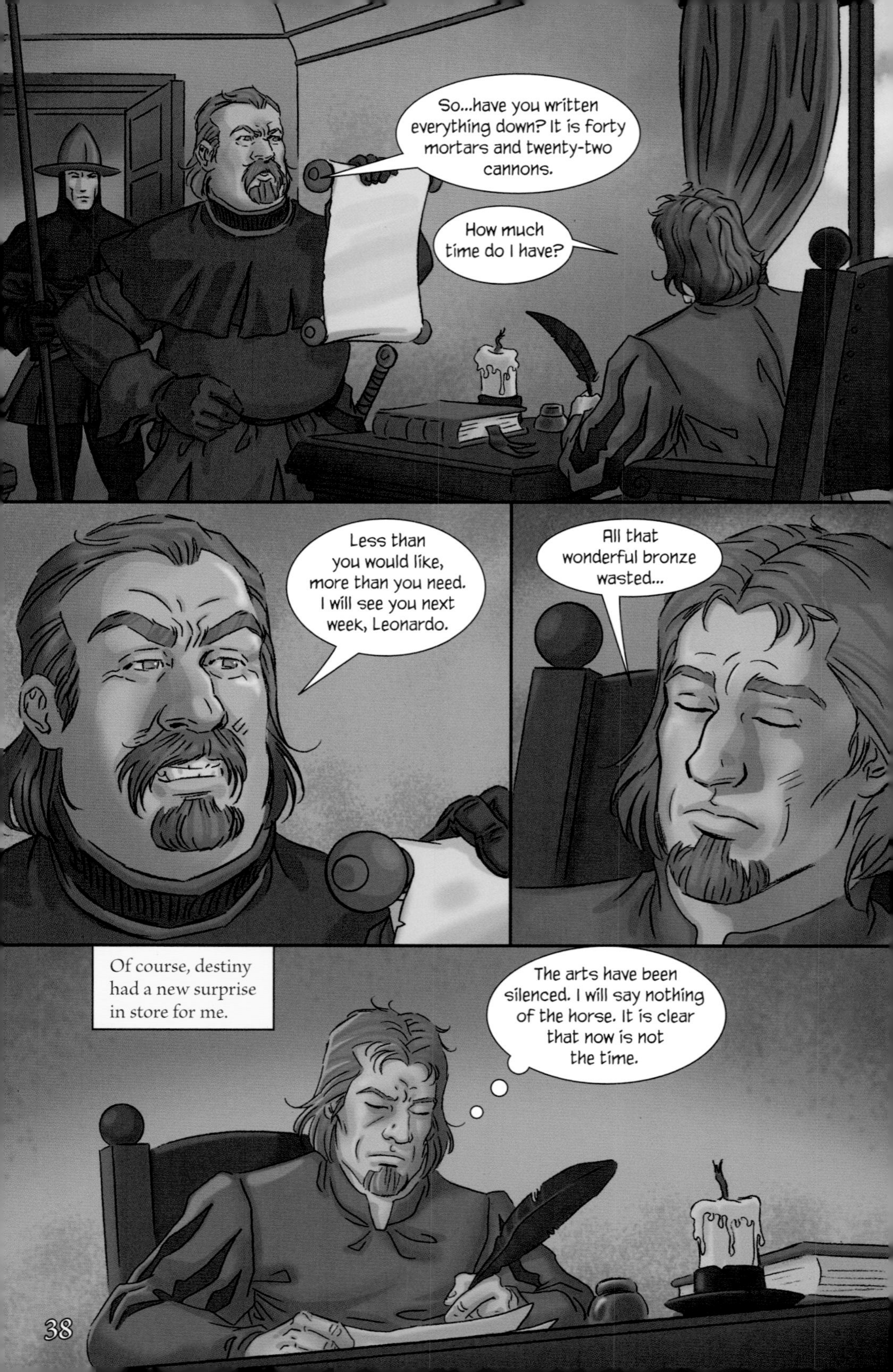
So...have you written everything down? It is forty mortars and twenty-two cannons.
How much time do I have?
Less than you would like, more than you need. I will see you next week, Leonardo.
All that wonderful bronze wasted...
Of course, destiny had a new surprise in store for me.
The arts have been silenced. I will say nothing of the horse. It is clear that now is not the time.

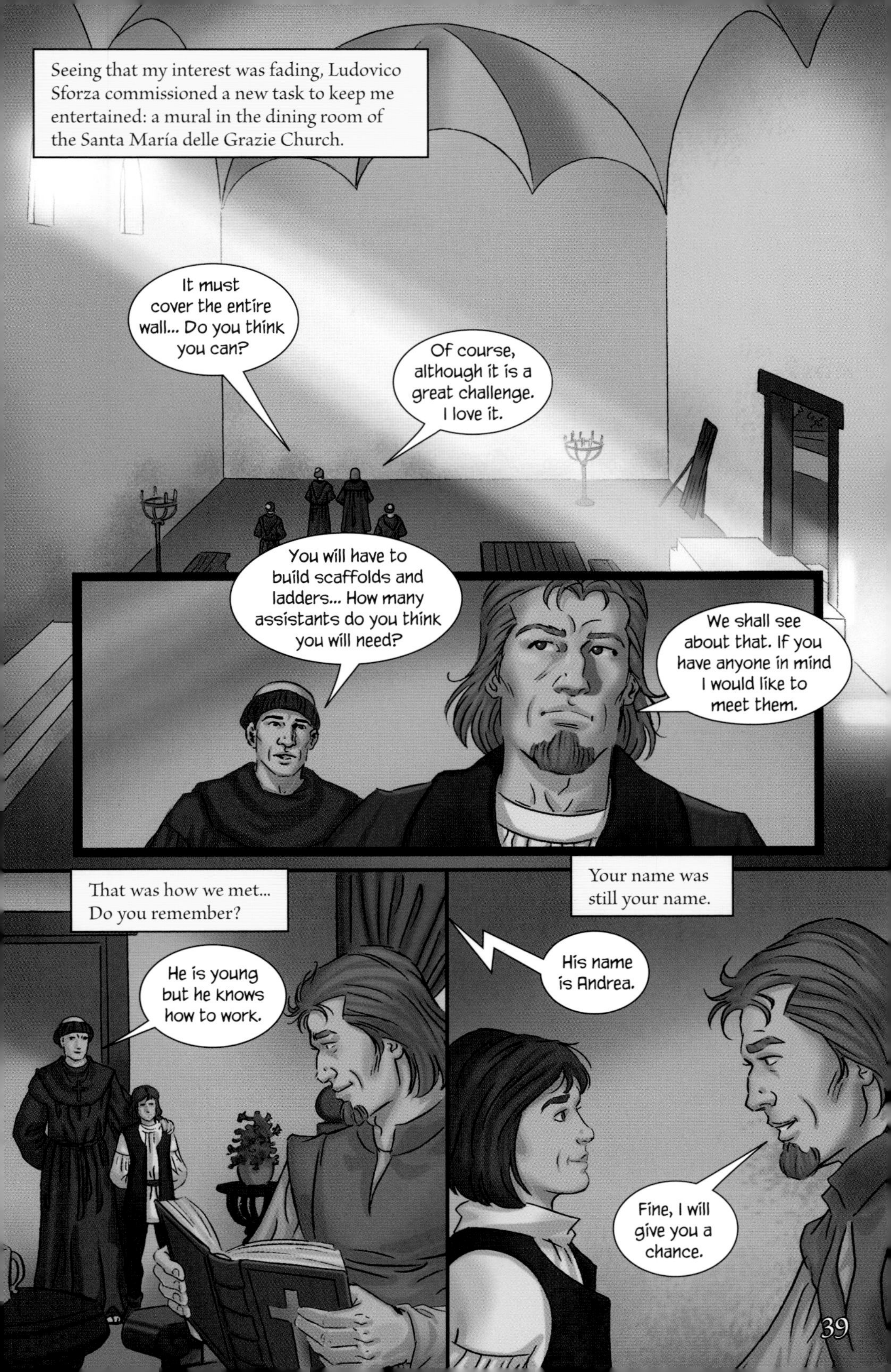
Seeing that my interest was fading, Ludovico Sforza commissioned a new task to keep me entertained: a mural in the dining room of the Santa María delle Grazie Church.
It must cover the entire wall... Do you think you can?
Of course, although it is a great challenge. I love it.
You will have to build scaffolds and ladders... How many assistants do you think you will need?
We shall see about that. If you have anyone in mind I would like to meet them.
That was how we met... Do you remember?
He is young but he knows how to work.
Your name was still your name.
His name is Andrea.
Fine, I will give you a chance.

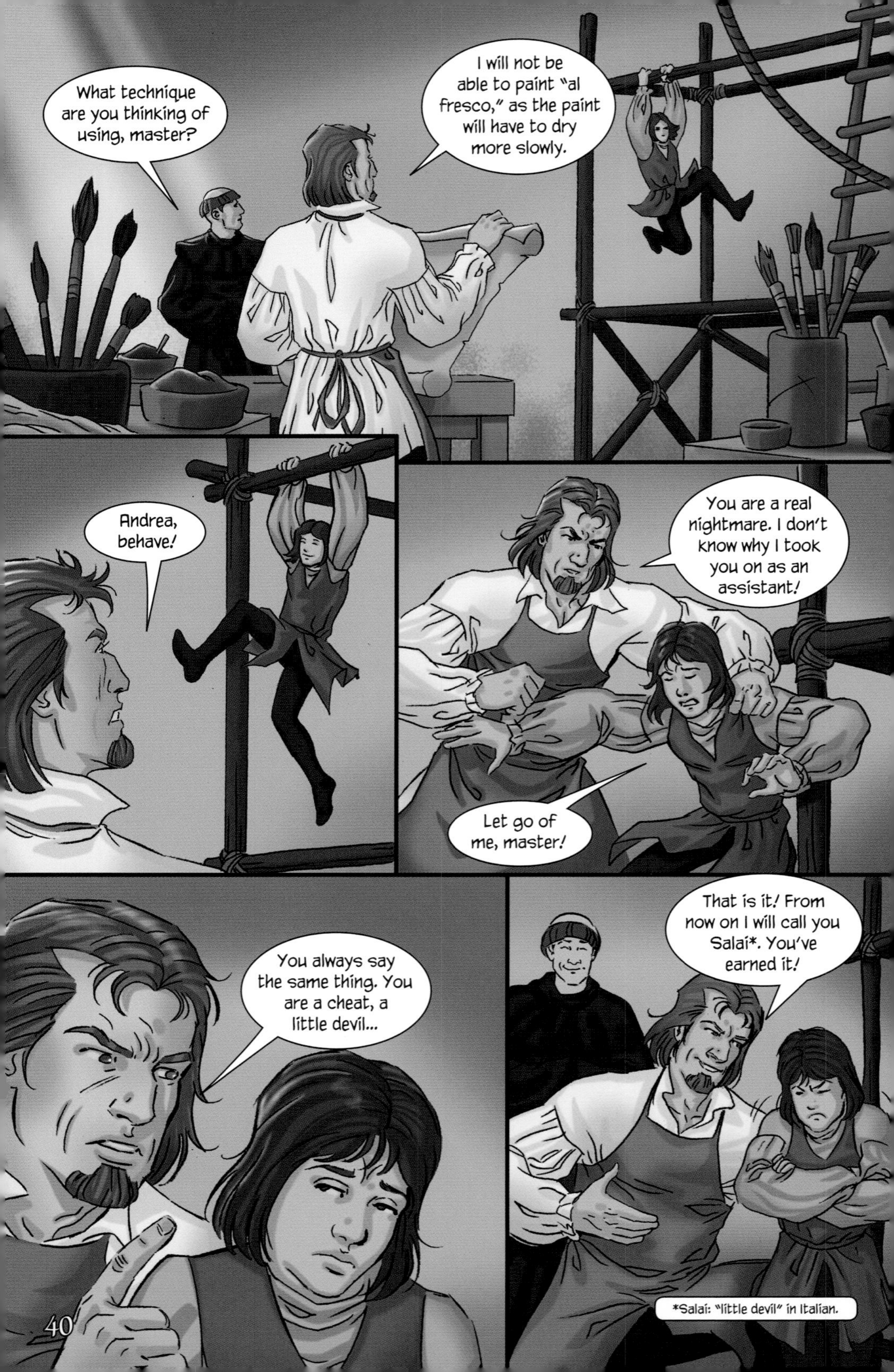
What technique are you thinking of using, master?
I will not be able to paint "al fresco," as the paint will have to dry more slowly.
Andrea, behave!
You are a real nightmare. I don't know why I took you on as an assistant!
Let go of me, master!
You always say the same thing. You are a cheat, a little devil...
That is it! From now on I will call you Salai*. You've earned it!
*Salai: "little devil" in Italian.

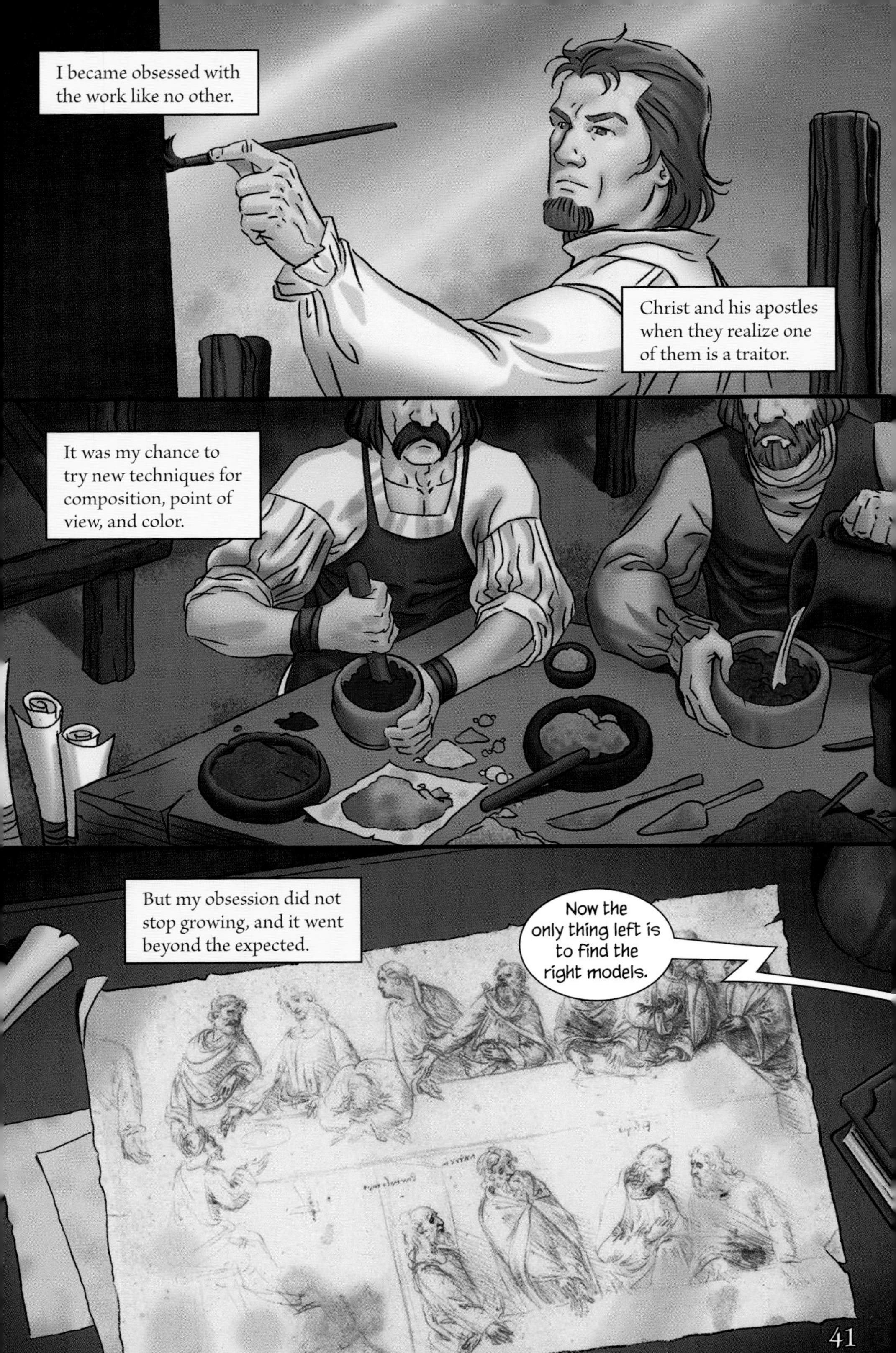
I became obsessed with the work like no other.
Christ and his apostles when they realize one of them is a traitor.
It was my chance to try new techniques for composition, point of view, and color.
But my obsession did not stop growing, and it went beyond the expected.
Now the only thing left is to find the right models.

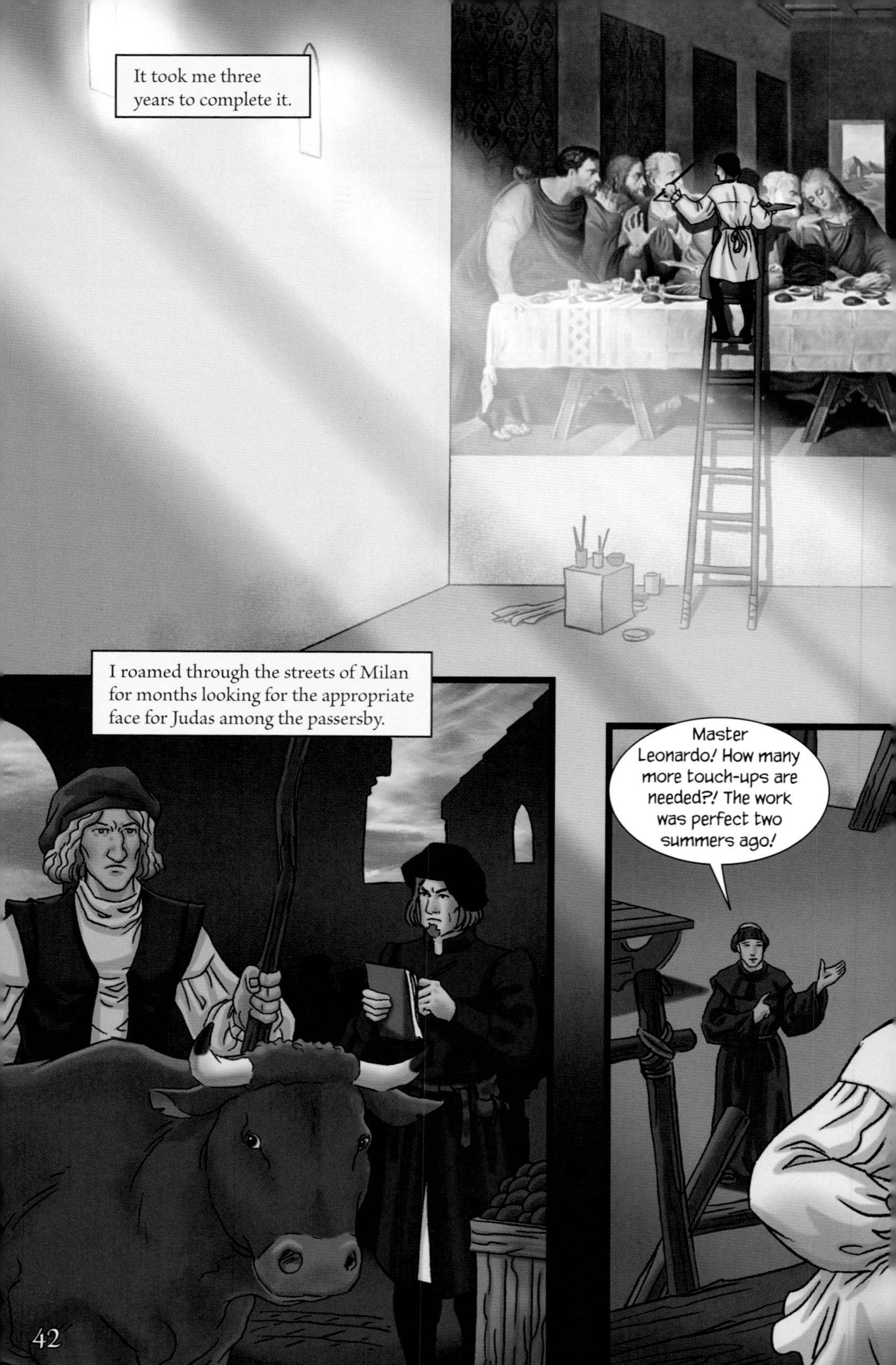
It took me three years to complete it.
I roamed through the streets of Milan for months looking for the appropriate face for Judas among the passersby.
Master Leonardo! How many more touch-ups are needed?! The work was perfect two summers ago!

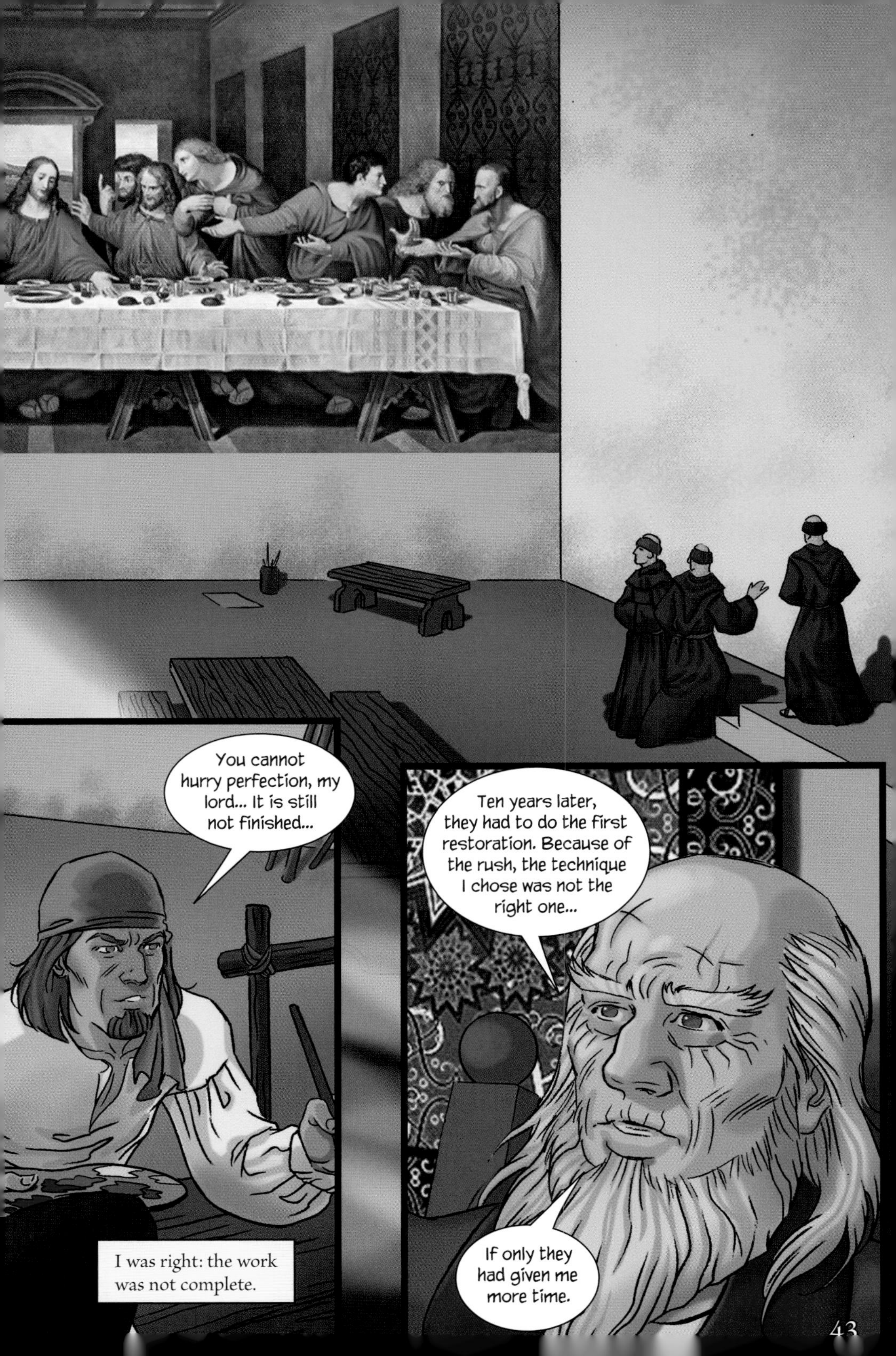

You cannot hurry perfection, my lord... It is still not finished...
I was right: the work was not complete.
Ten years later, they had to do the first restoration. Because of the rush, the technique I chose was not the right one...
If only they had given me more time.

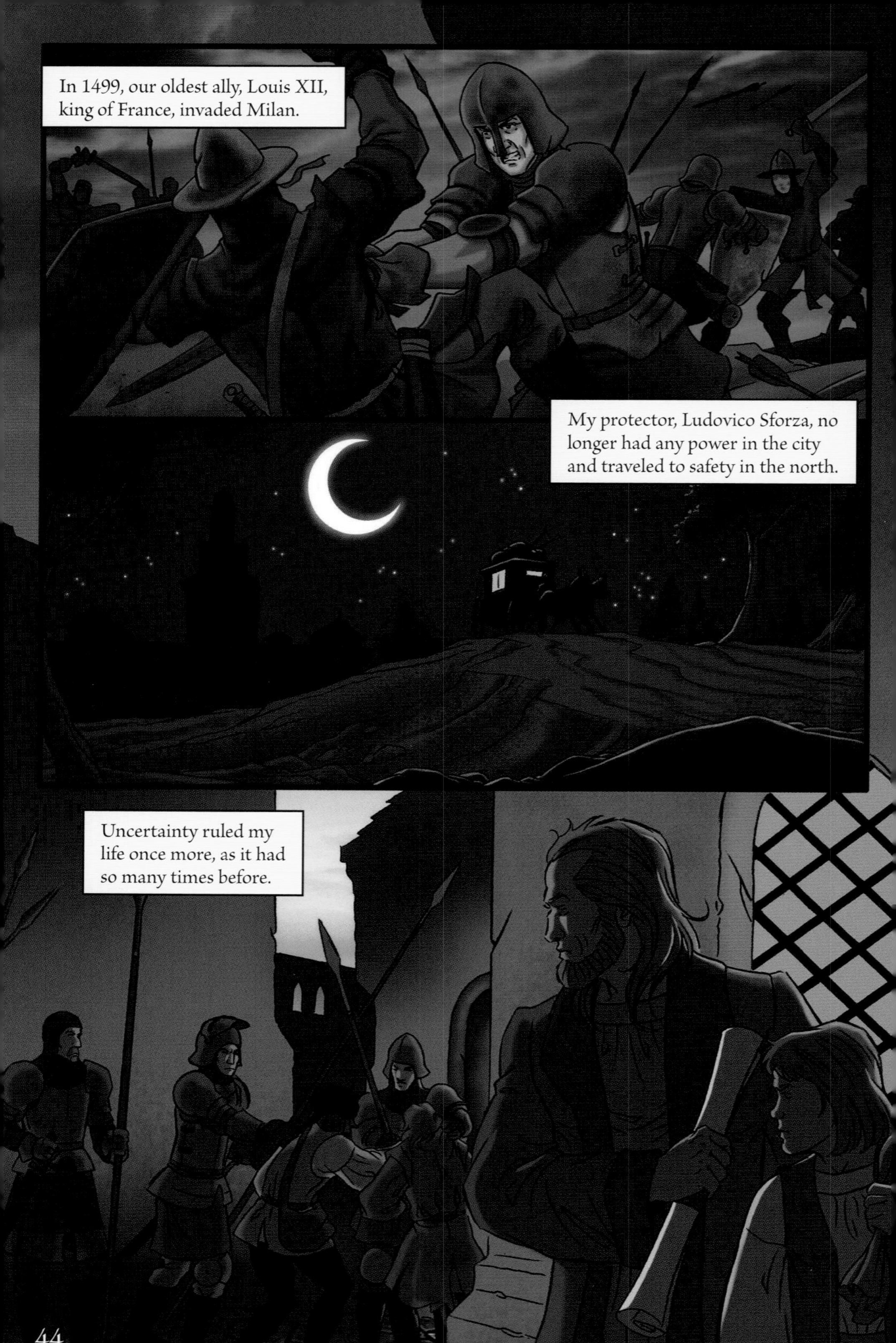
In 1499, our oldest ally, Louis XII, king of France, invaded Milan.
My protector, Ludovico Sforza, no longer had any power in the city and traveled to safety in the north.
Uncertainty ruled my life once more, as it had so many times before.

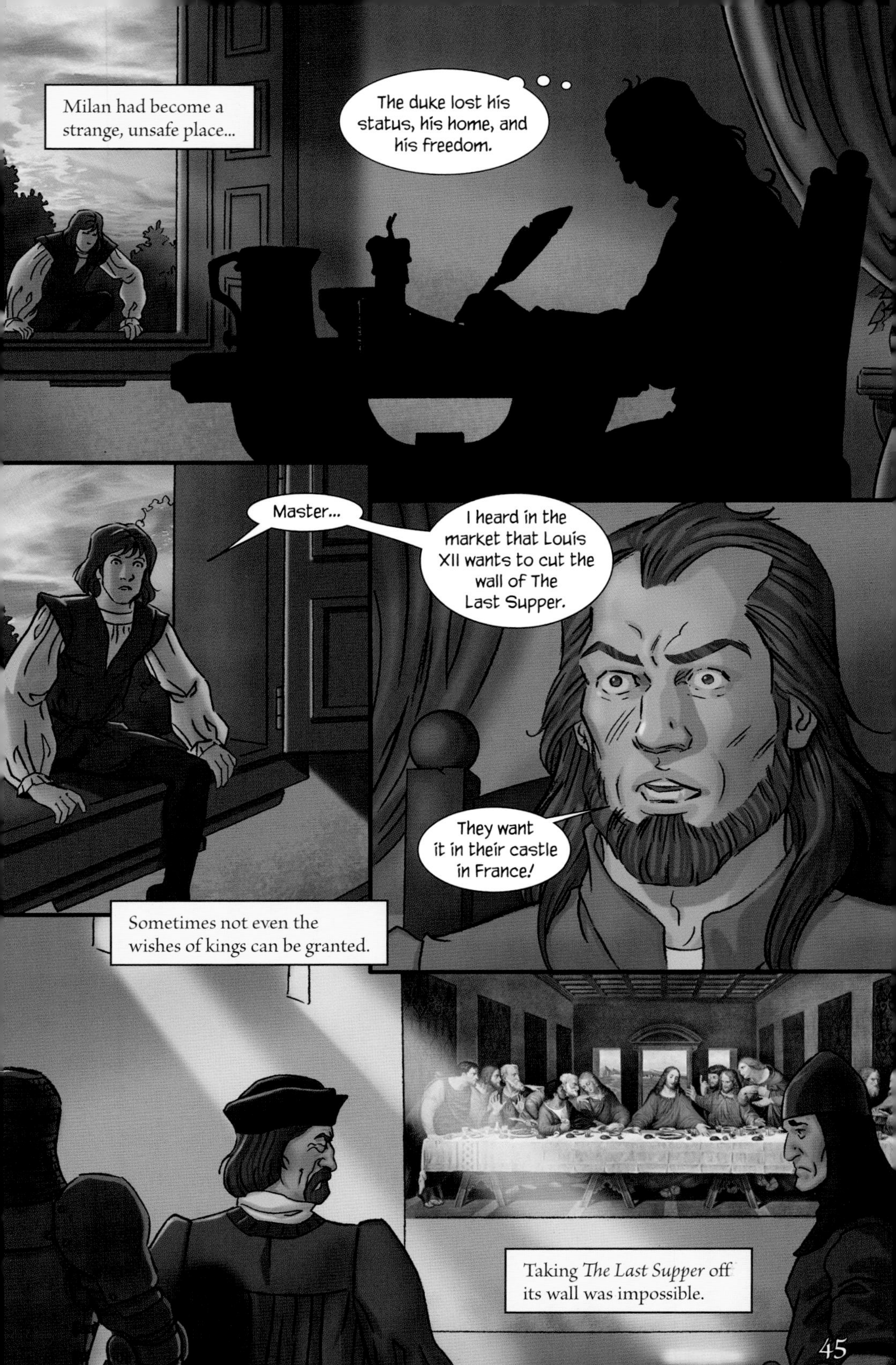
Milan had become a strange, unsafe place...
The duke lost his status, his home, and his freedom.
Master...
I heard in the market that Louis XII wants to cut the wall of The Last Supper.
They want it in their castle in France!
Sometimes not even the wishes of kings can be granted.
Taking *The Last Supper* off its wall was impossible.

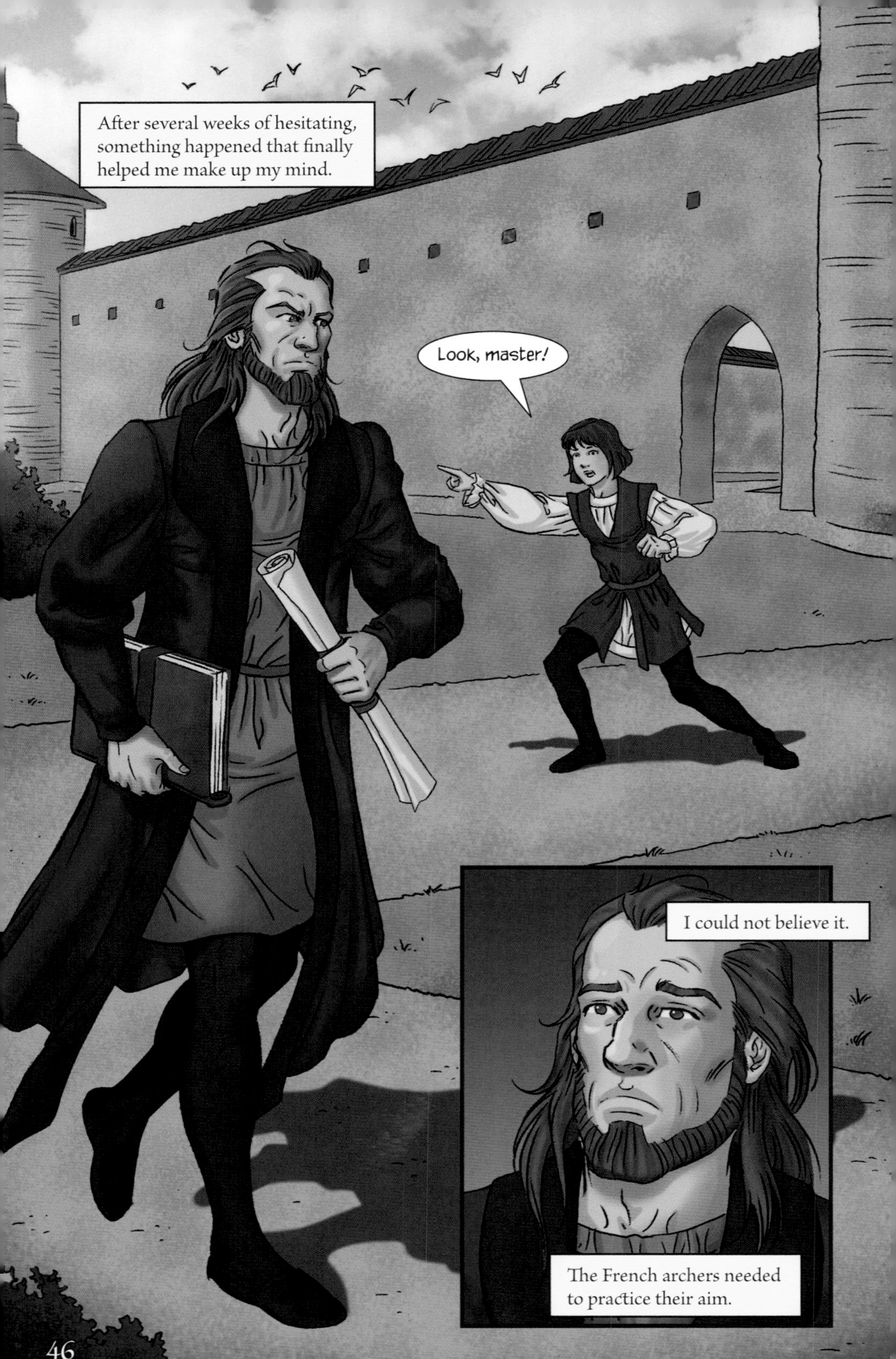
After several weeks of hesitating, something happened that finally helped me make up my mind.
Look, master!
I could not believe it.
The French archers needed to practice their aim.

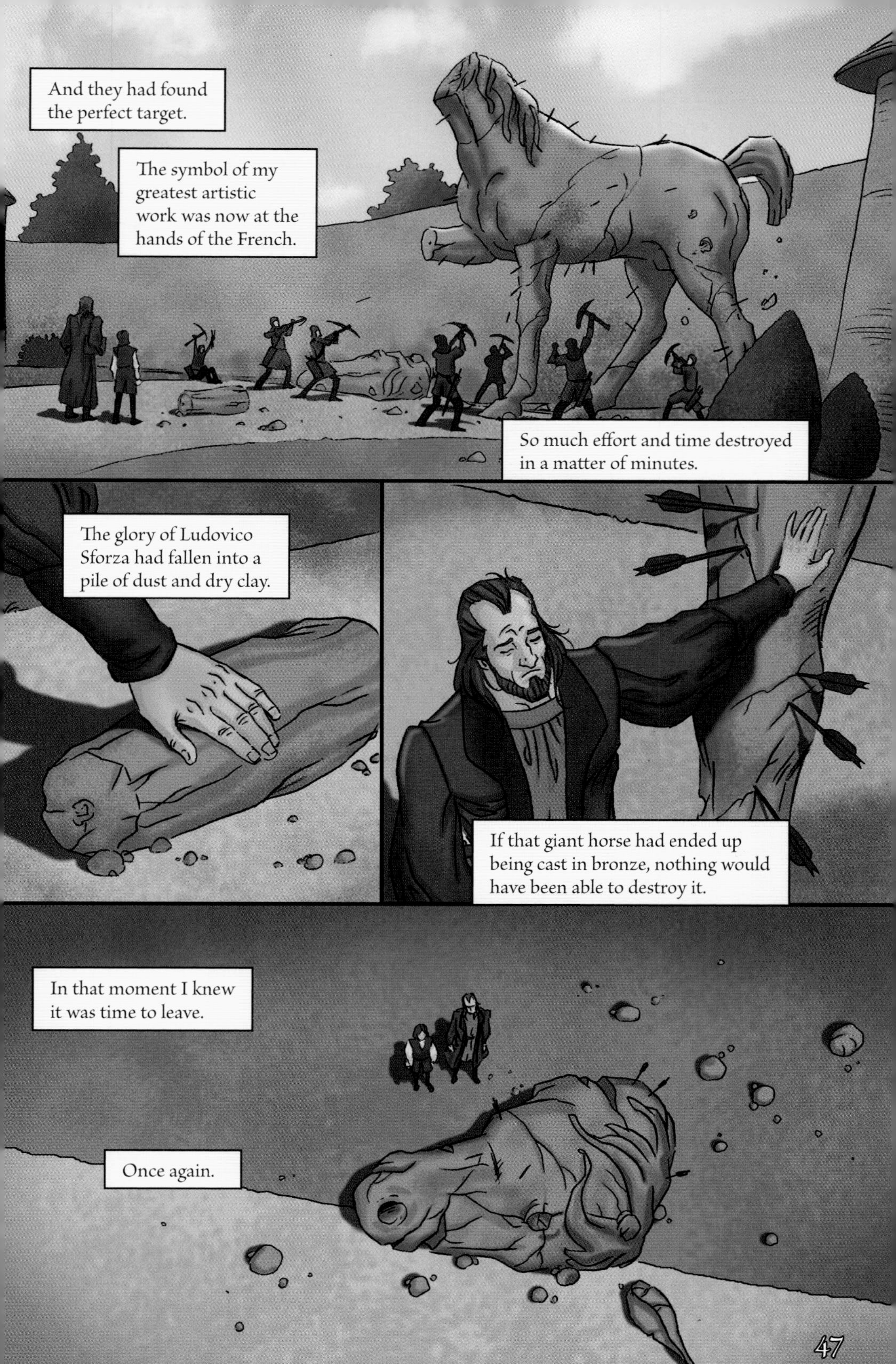
And they had found the perfect target.
The symbol of my greatest artistic work was now at the hands of the French.
So much effort and time destroyed in a matter of minutes.
The glory of Ludovico Sforza had fallen into a pile of dust and dry clay.
If that giant horse had ended up being cast in bronze, nothing would have been able to destroy it.
In that moment I knew it was time to leave.
Once again.

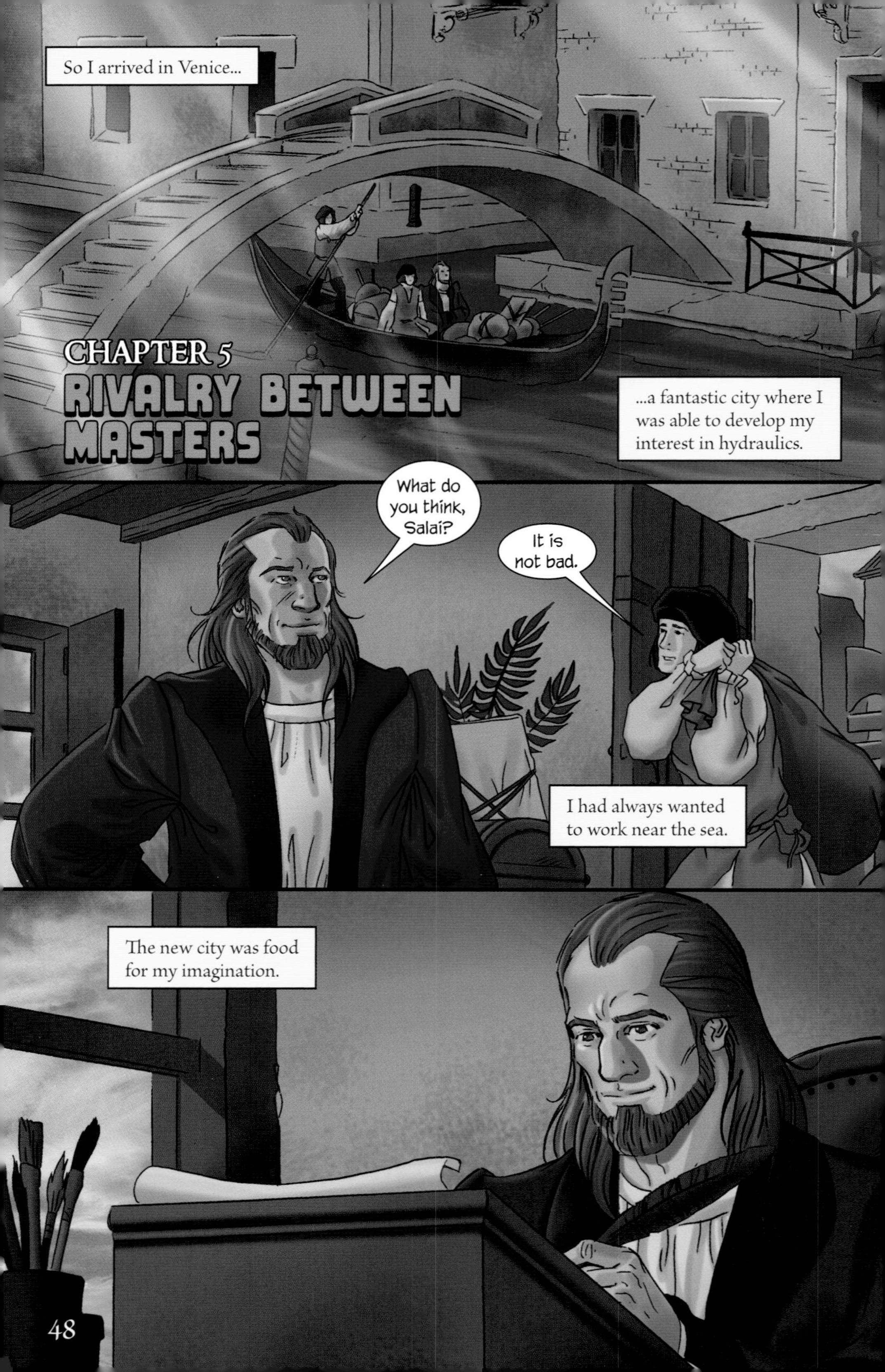
So I arrived in Venice...
CHAPTER 5
RIVALRY BETWEEN MASTERS
...a fantastic city where I was able to develop my interest in hydraulics.
What do you think, Salai?
It is not bad.
I had always wanted to work near the sea.
The new city was food for my imagination.

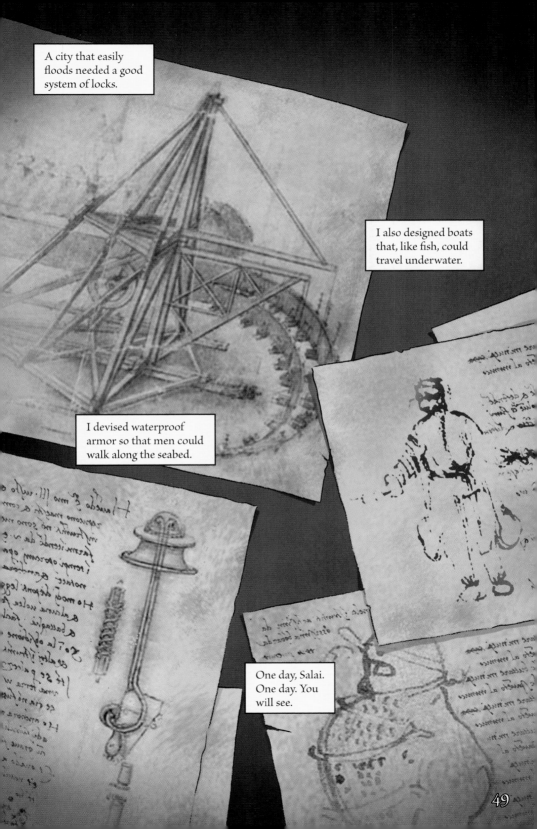

A city that easily floods needed a good system of locks.

I also designed boats that, like fish, could travel underwater.

I devised waterproof armor so that men could walk along the seabed.

One day, Salai. One day. You will see.

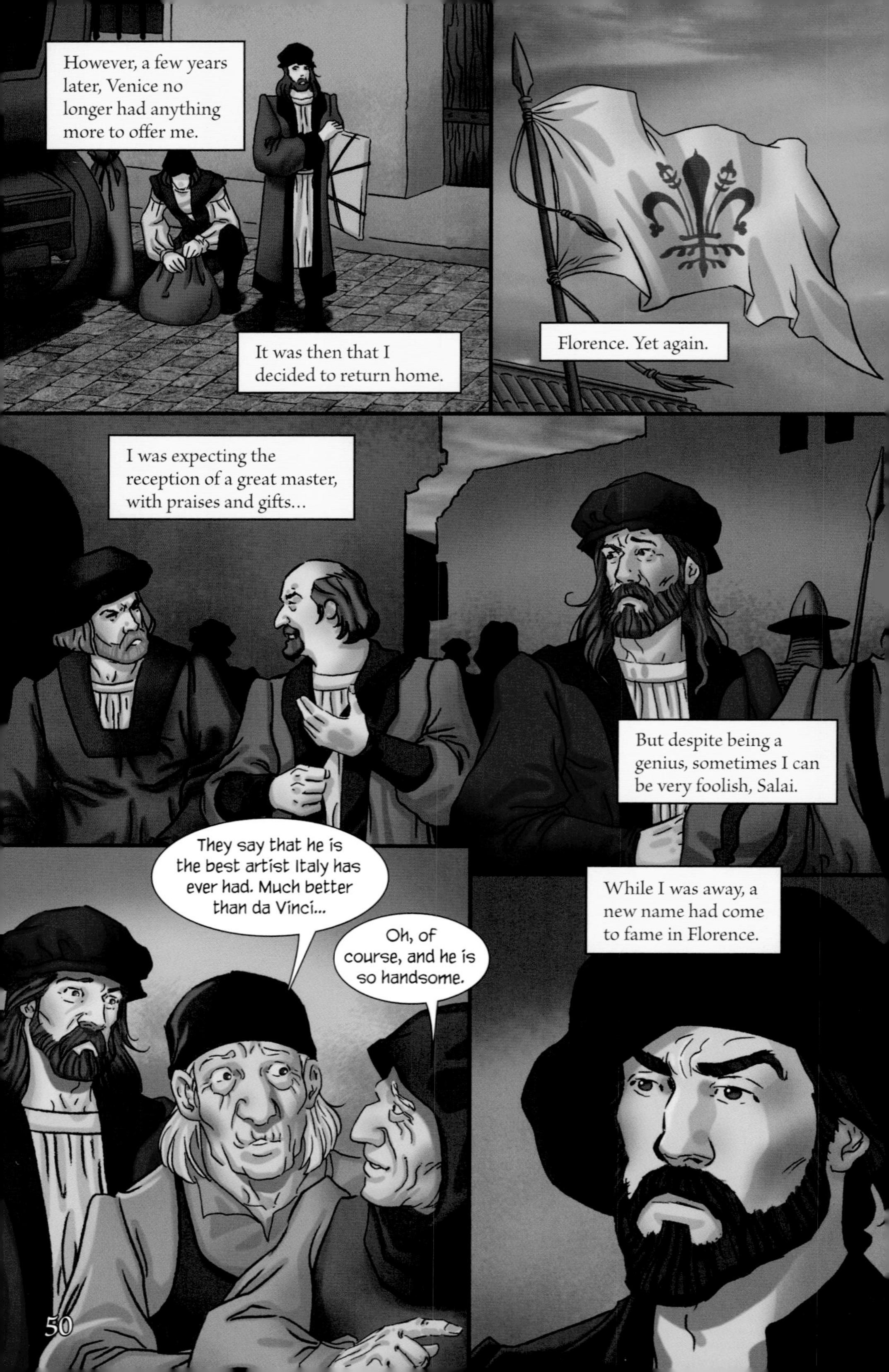
However, a few years later, Venice no longer had anything more to offer me.
It was then that I decided to return home.
Florence. Yet again.
I was expecting the reception of a great master, with praises and gifts...
But despite being a genius, sometimes I can be very foolish, Salai.
They say that he is the best artist Italy has ever had. Much better than da Vinci...
Oh, of course, and he is so handsome.
While I was away, a new name had come to fame in Florence.

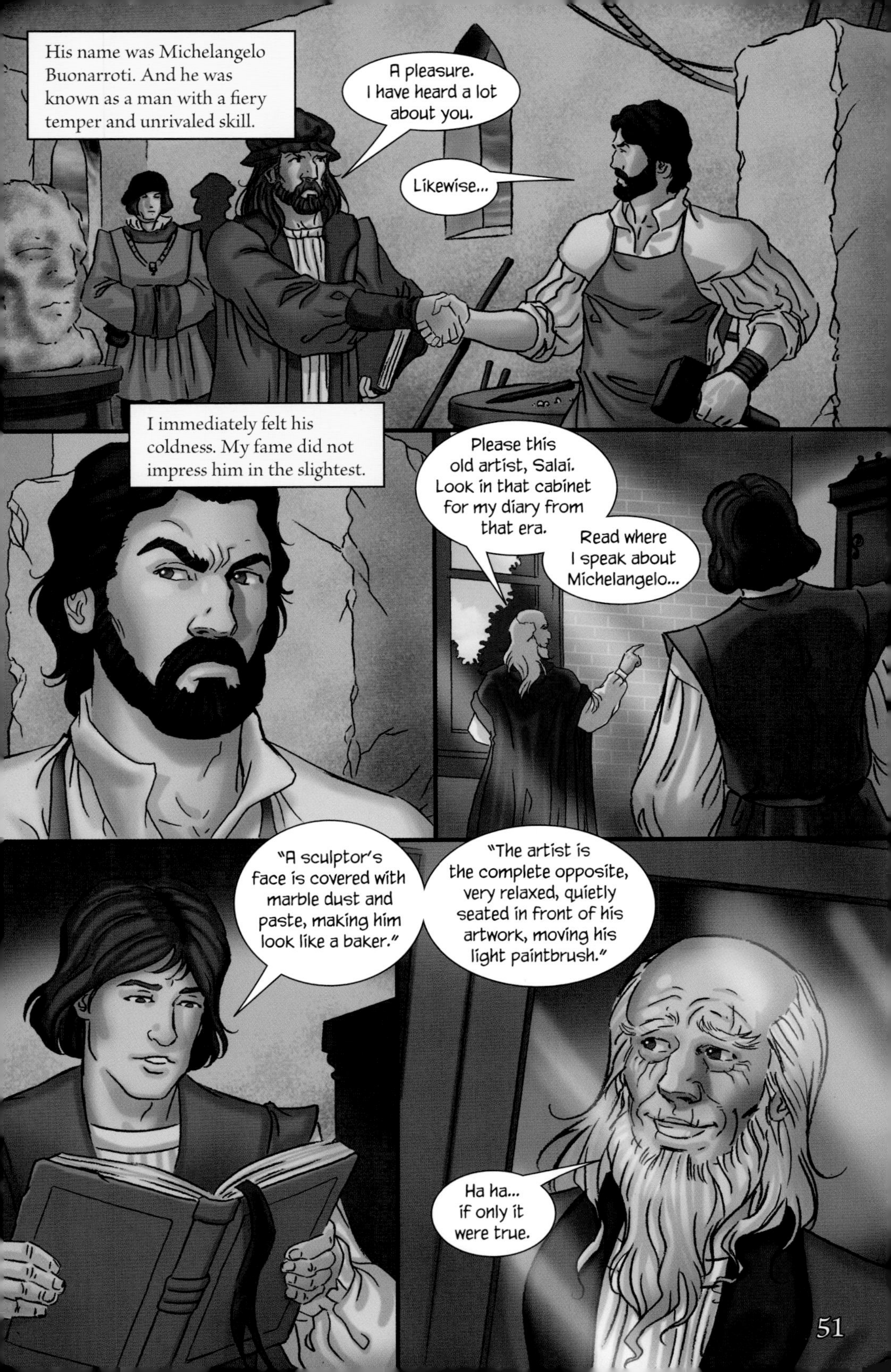
His name was Michelangelo Buonarroti. And he was known as a man with a fiery temper and unrivaled skill.
A pleasure. I have heard a lot about you.
Likewise...
I immediately felt his coldness. My fame did not impress him in the slightest.
Please this old artist, Salai. Look in that cabinet for my diary from that era.
Read where I speak about Michelangelo...
"A sculptor's face is covered with marble dust and paste, making him look like a baker."
"The artist is the complete opposite, very relaxed, quietly seated in front of his artwork, moving his light paintbrush."
Ha ha... if only it were true.

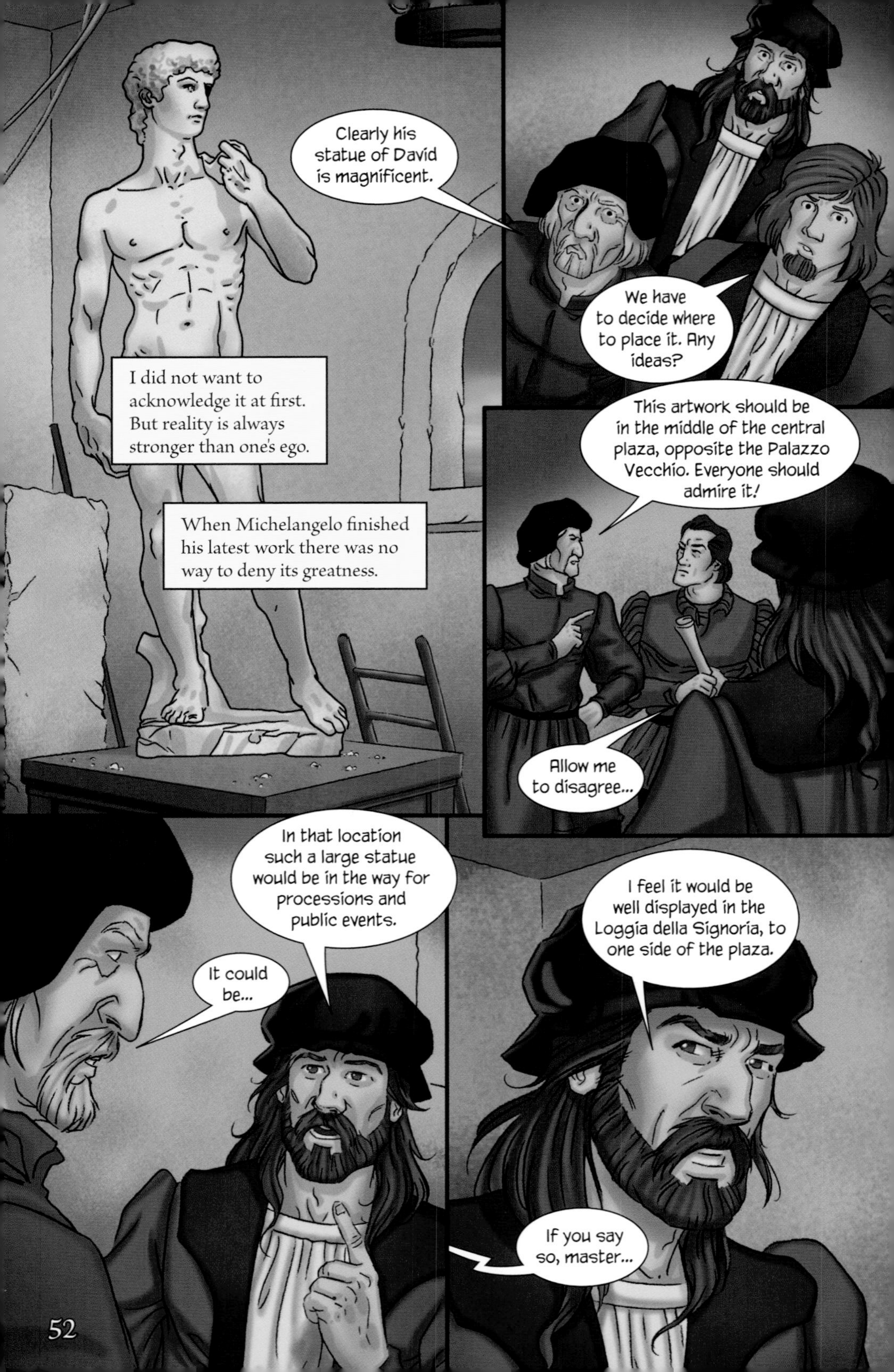

I did not want to acknowledge it at first. But reality is always stronger than one's ego.
When Michelangelo finished his latest work there was no way to deny its greatness.
Clearly his statue of David is magnificent.
We have to decide where to place it. Any ideas?
This artwork should be in the middle of the central plaza, opposite the Palazzo Vecchio. Everyone should admire it!
Allow me to disagree...
In that location such a large statue would be in the way for processions and public events.
It could be...
I feel it would be well displayed in the Loggia della Signoria, to one side of the plaza.
If you say so, master...

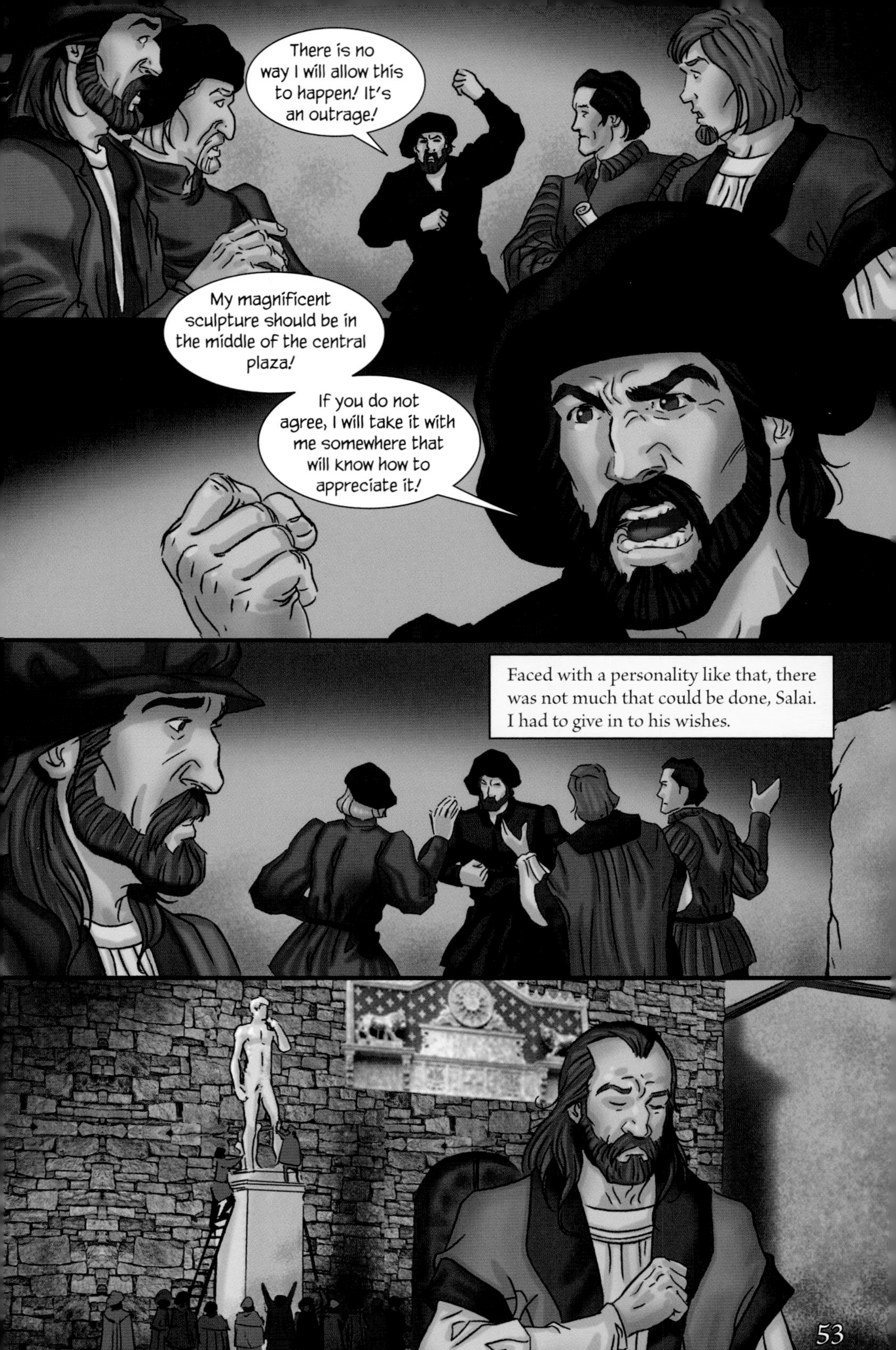
There is no way I will allow this to happen! It's an outrage!
My magnificent sculpture should be in the middle of the central plaza!
If you do not agree, I will take it with me somewhere that will know how to appreciate it!
Faced with a personality like that, there was not much that could be done, Salai. I had to give in to his wishes.

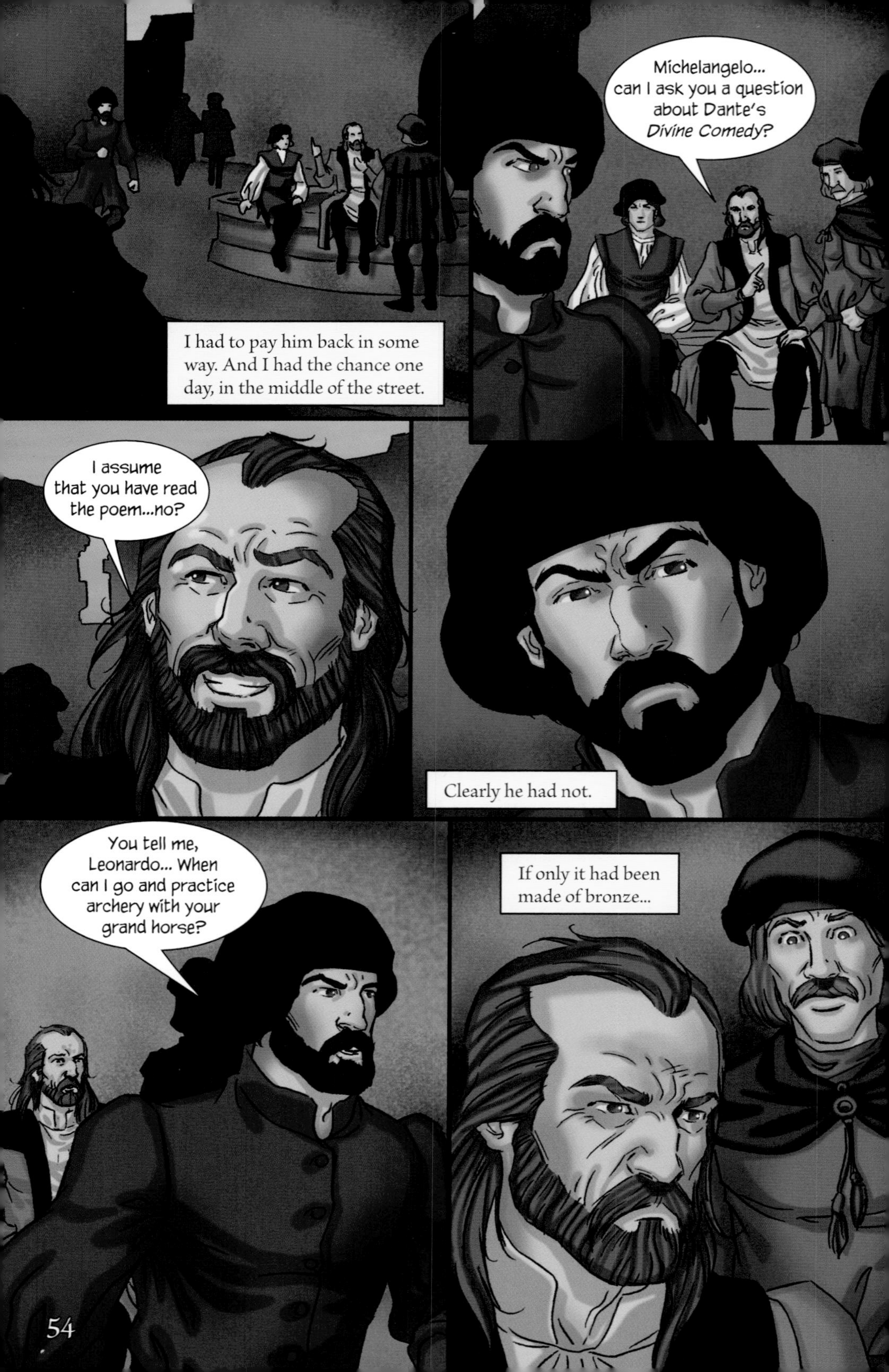
I had to pay him back in some way. And I had the chance one day, in the middle of the street.
Michelangelo... can I ask you a question about Dante's *Divine Comedy*?
I assume that you have read the poem...no?
Clearly he had not.
You tell me, Leonardo... When can I go and practice archery with your grand horse?
If only it had been made of bronze...

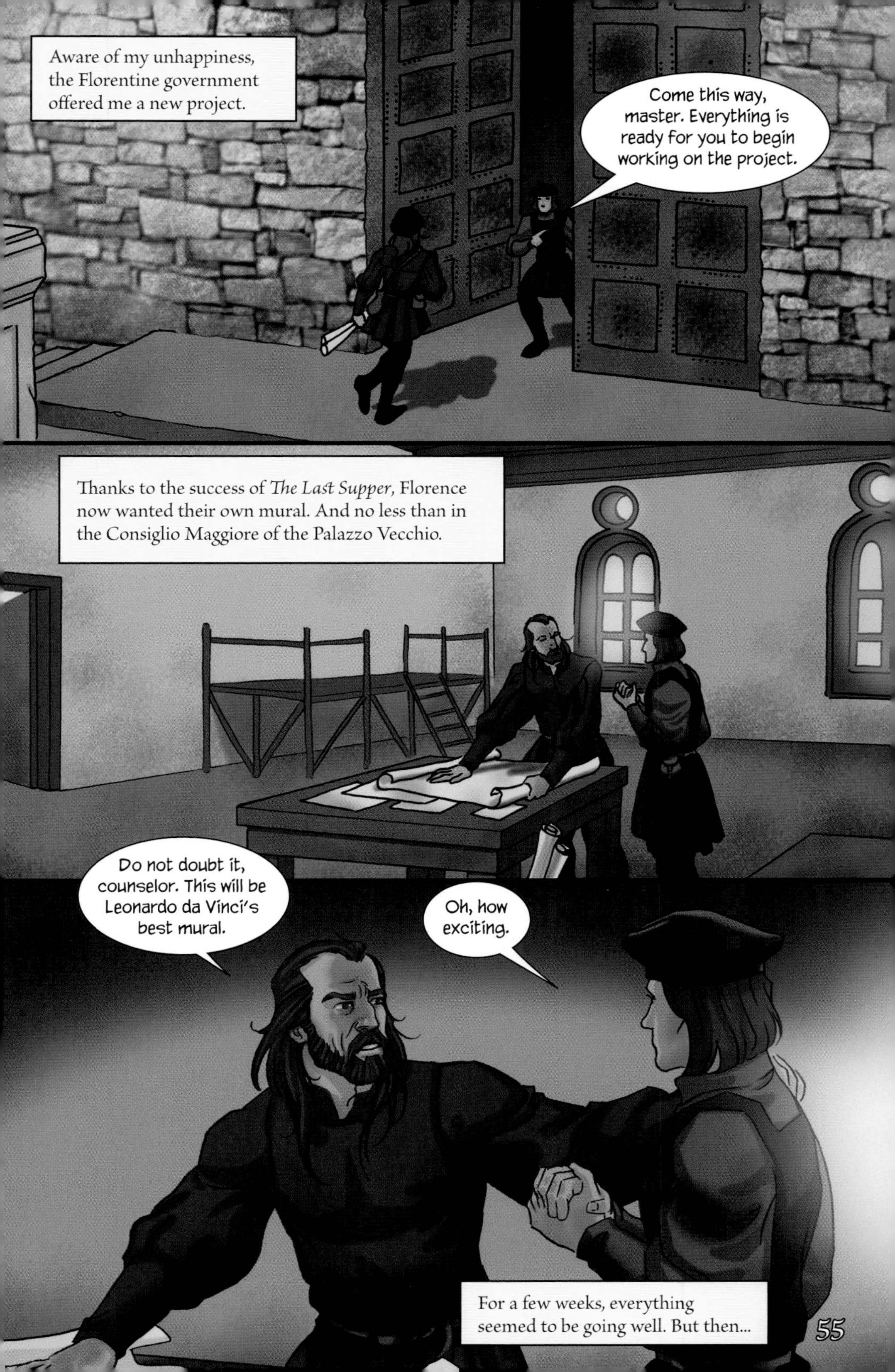
Aware of my unhappiness, the Florentine government offered me a new project.
Come this way, master. Everything is ready for you to begin working on the project.
Thanks to the success of *The Last Supper,* Florence now wanted their own mural. And no less than in the Consiglio Maggiore of the Palazzo Vecchio.
Do not doubt it, counselor. This will be Leonardo da Vinci's best mural.
Oh, how exciting.
For a few weeks, everything seemed to be going well. But then...

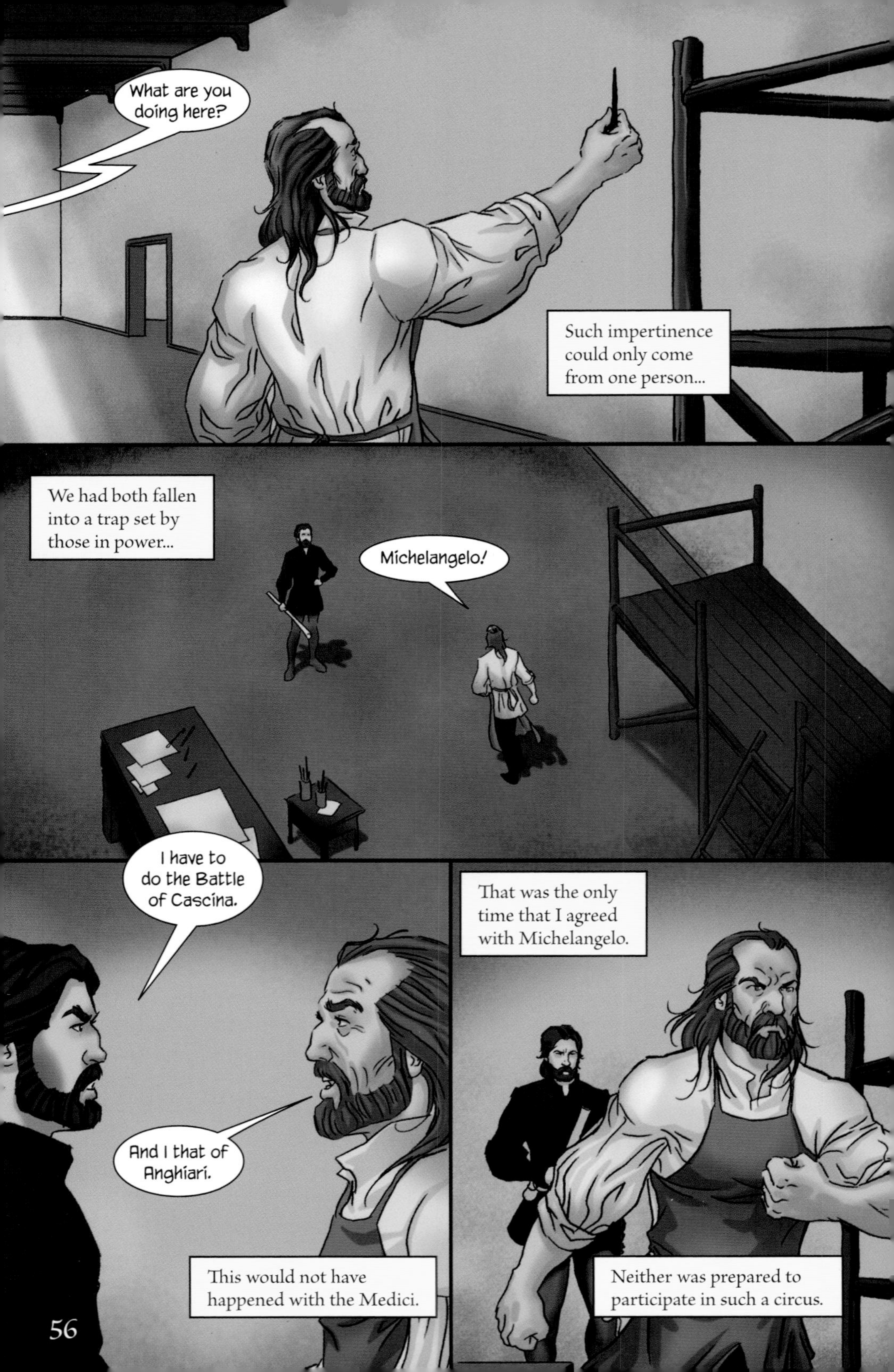
What are you doing here?
Such impertinence could only come from one person...
We had both fallen into a trap set by those in power...
Michelangelo!
I have to do the Battle of Cascina.
And I that of Anghiari.
This would not have happened with the Medici.
That was the only time that I agreed with Michelangelo.
Neither was prepared to participate in such a circus.

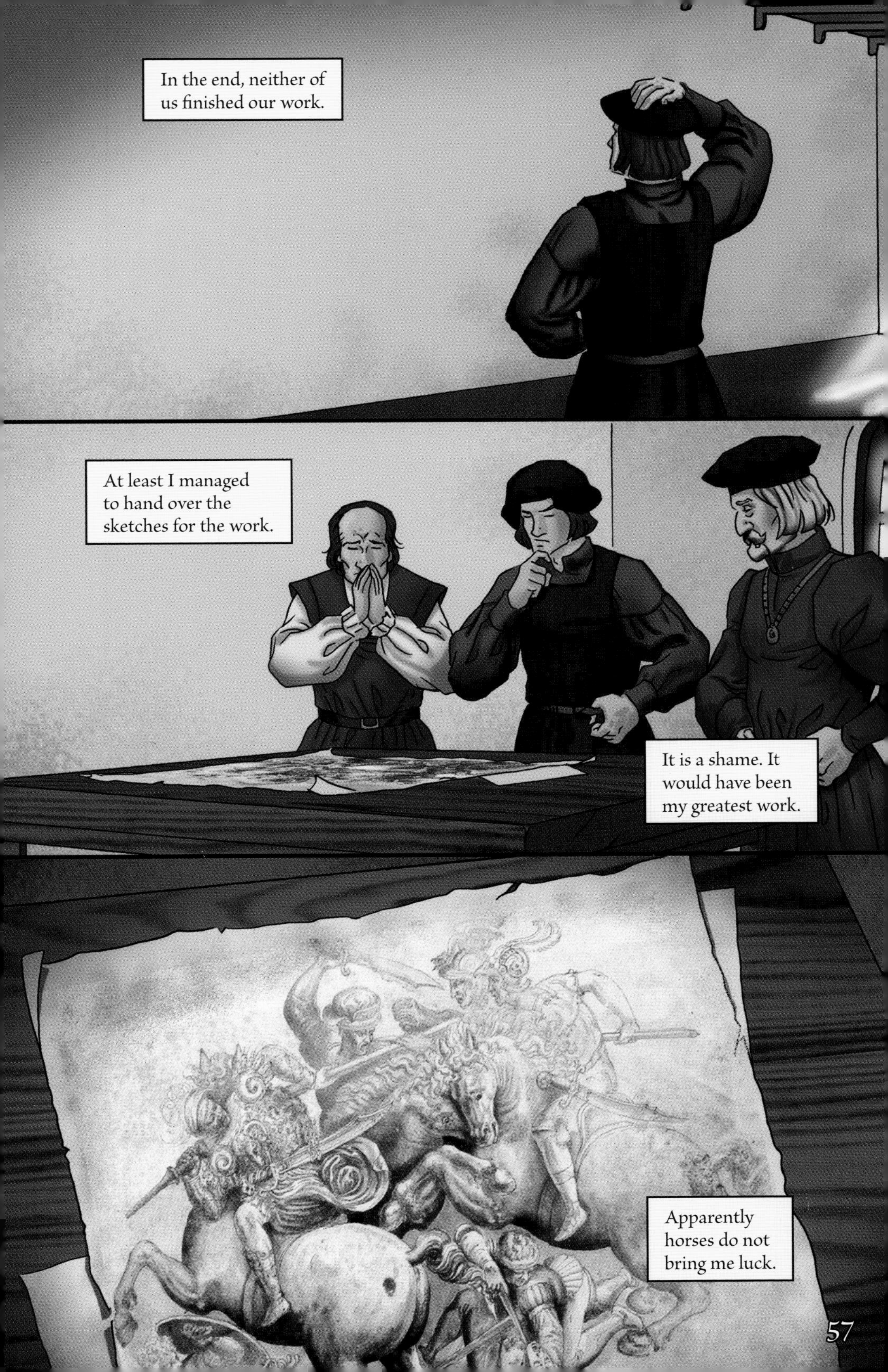
In the end, neither of us finished our work.
At least I managed to hand over the sketches for the work.
It is a shame. It would have been my greatest work.
Apparently horses do not bring me luck.

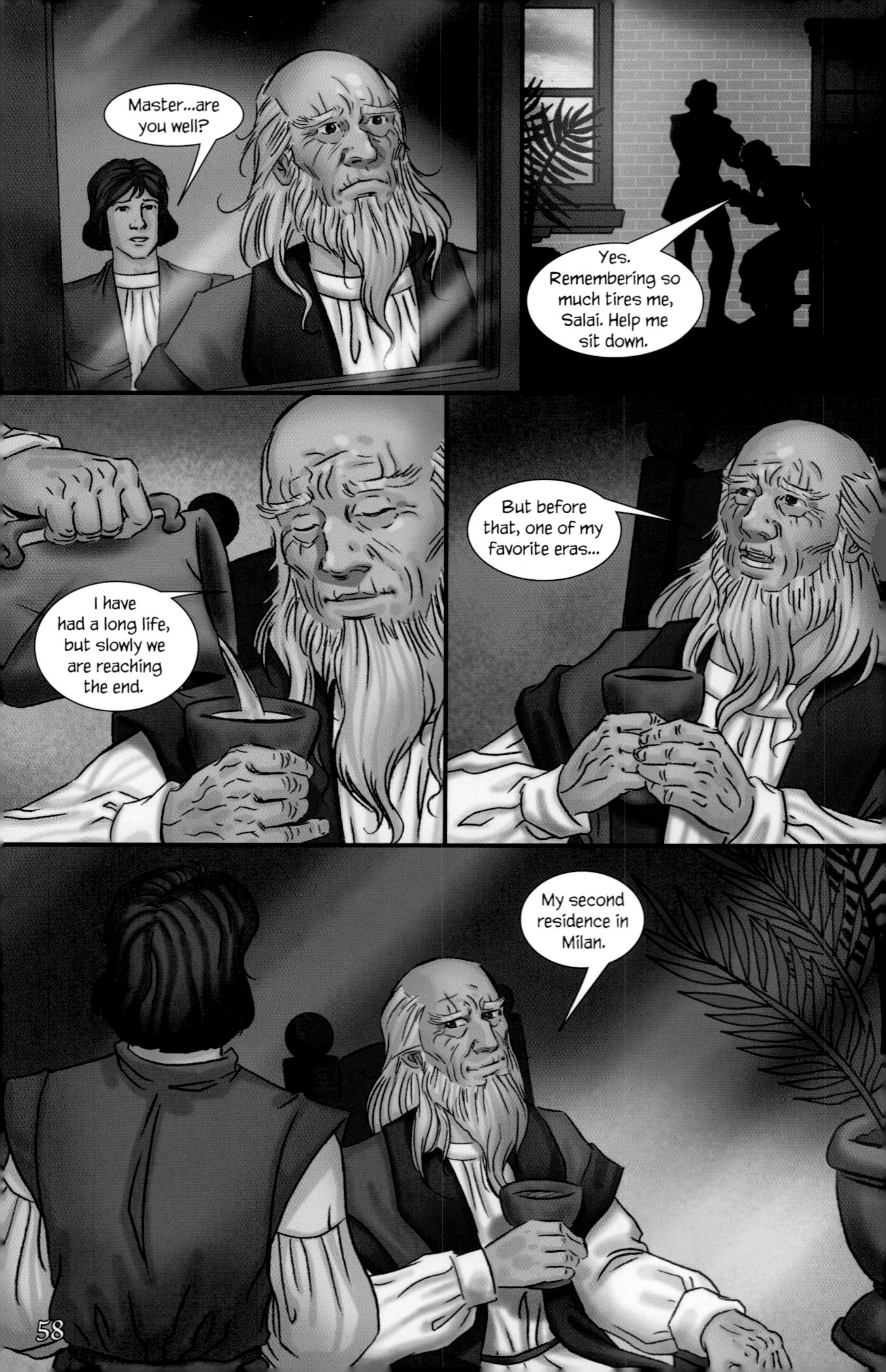
Master...are you well?
Yes. Remembering so much tires me, Salai. Help me sit down.
I have had a long life, but slowly we are reaching the end.
But before that, one of my favorite eras...
My second residence in Milan.

CHAPTER 6
LEONARDO'S LEGACY

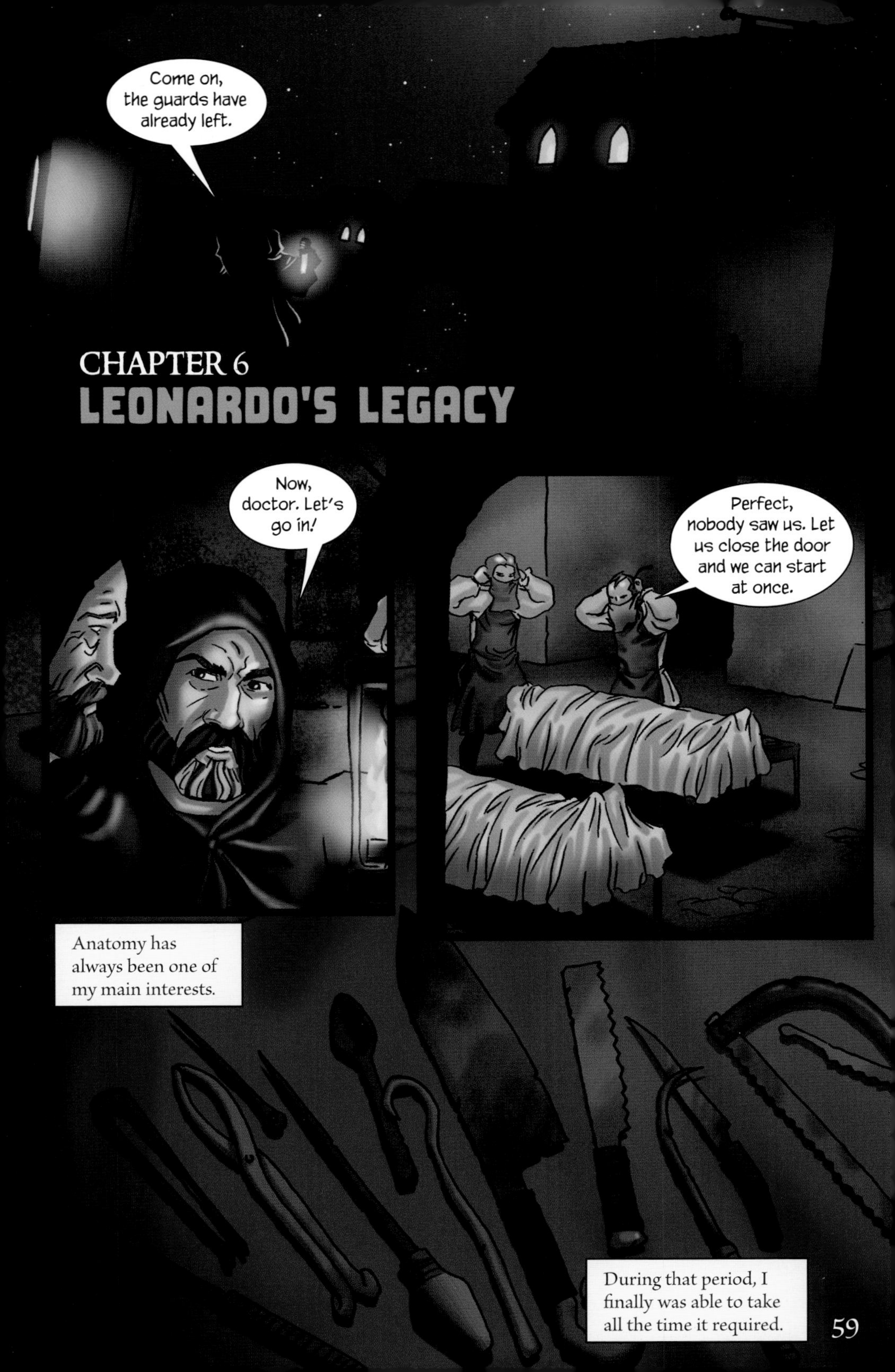

Come on, the guards have already left.
Now, doctor. Let's go in!
Perfect, nobody saw us. Let us close the door and we can start at once.
Anatomy has always been one of my main interests.
During that period, I finally was able to take all the time it required.

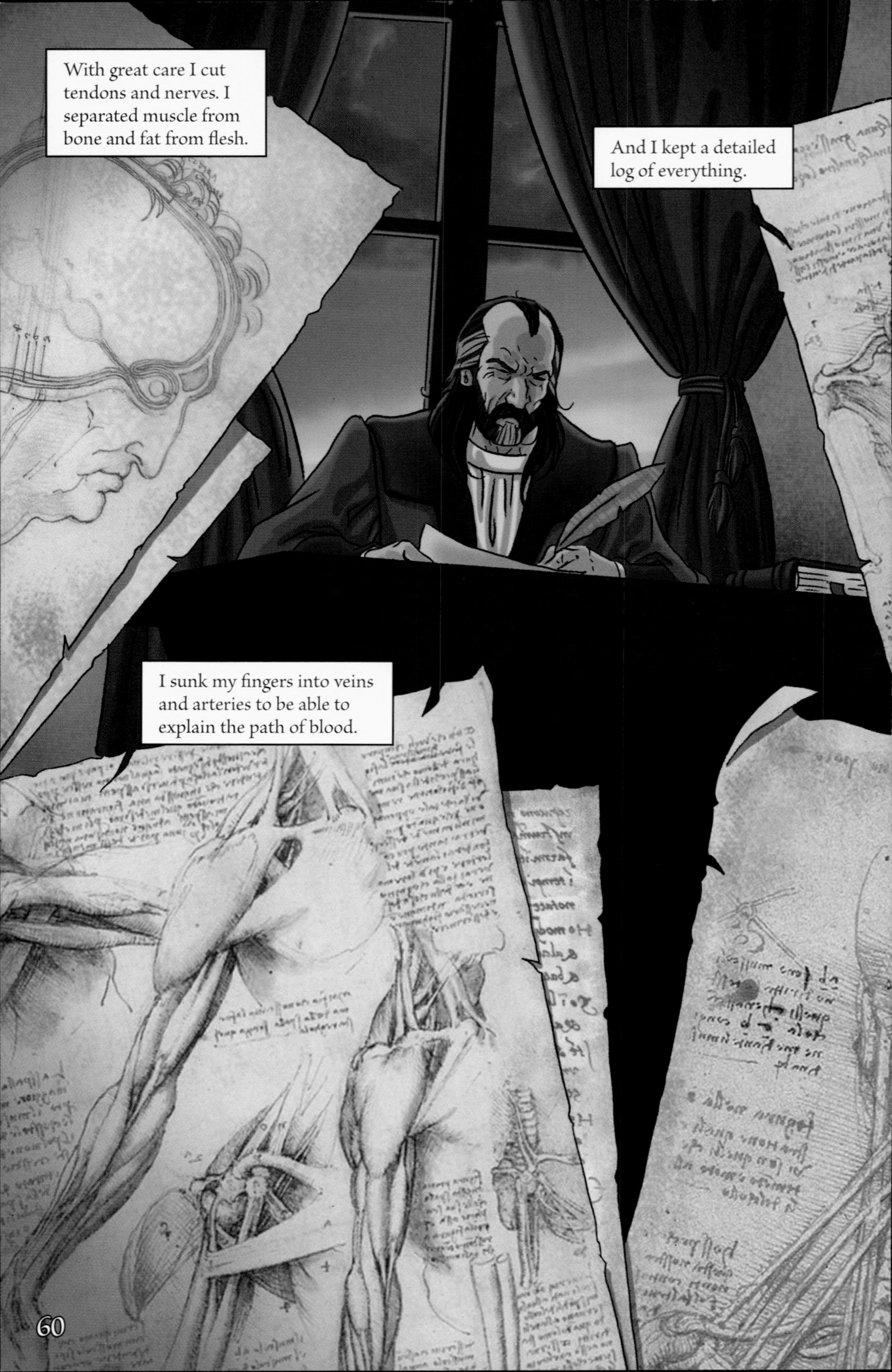
With great care I cut tendons and nerves. I separated muscle from bone and fat from flesh.
And I kept a detailed log of everything.
I sunk my fingers into veins and arteries to be able to explain the path of blood.

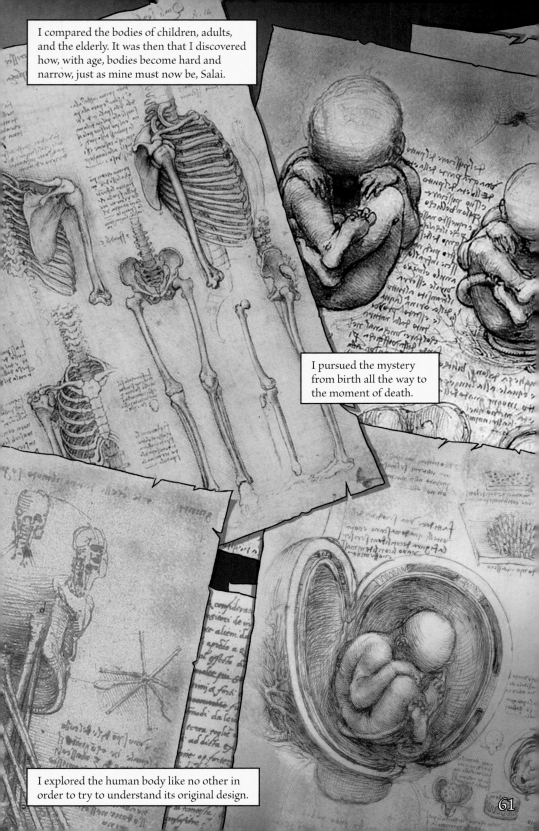

I compared the bodies of children, adults, and the elderly. It was then that I discovered how, with age, bodies become hard and narrow, just as mine must now be, Salai.

I pursued the mystery from birth all the way to the moment of death.

I explored the human body like no other in order to try to understand its original design.

61

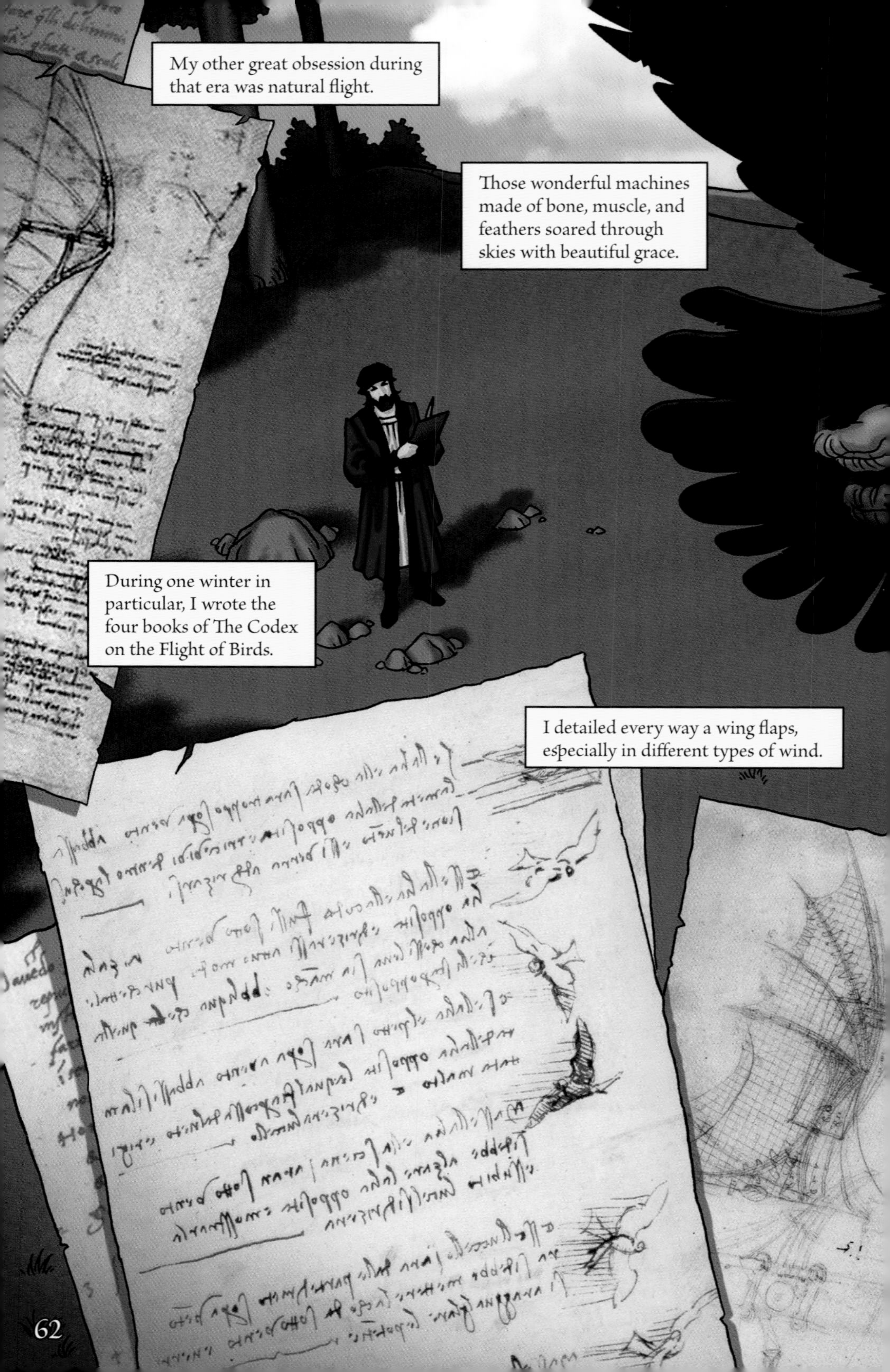
My other great obsession during that era was natural flight.
Those wonderful machines made of bone, muscle, and feathers soared through skies with beautiful grace.
During one winter in particular, I wrote the four books of The Codex on the Flight of Birds.
I detailed every way a wing flaps, especially in different types of wind.

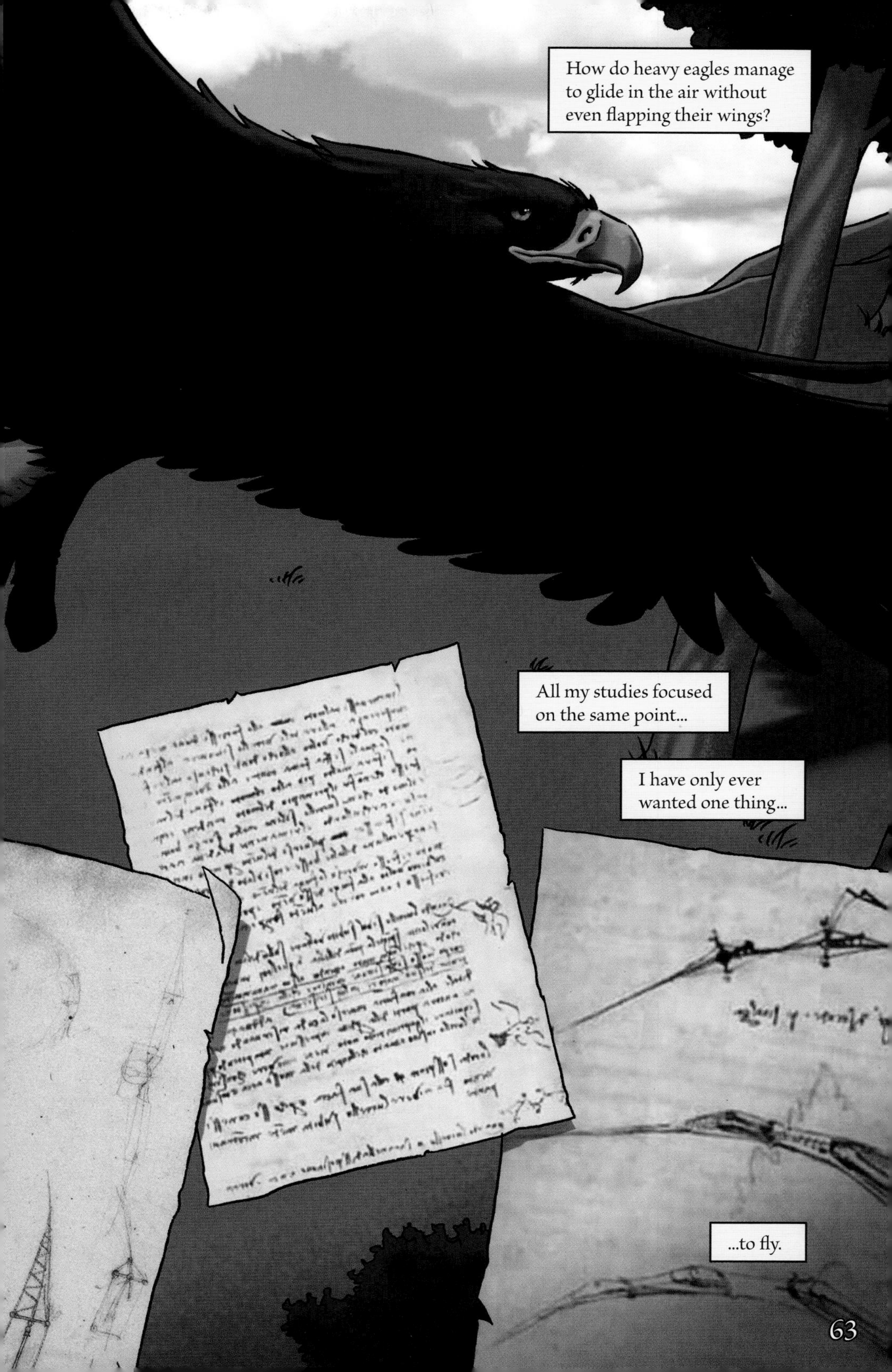
How do heavy eagles manage to glide in the air without even flapping their wings?
All my studies focused on the same point...
I have only ever wanted one thing...
...to fly.

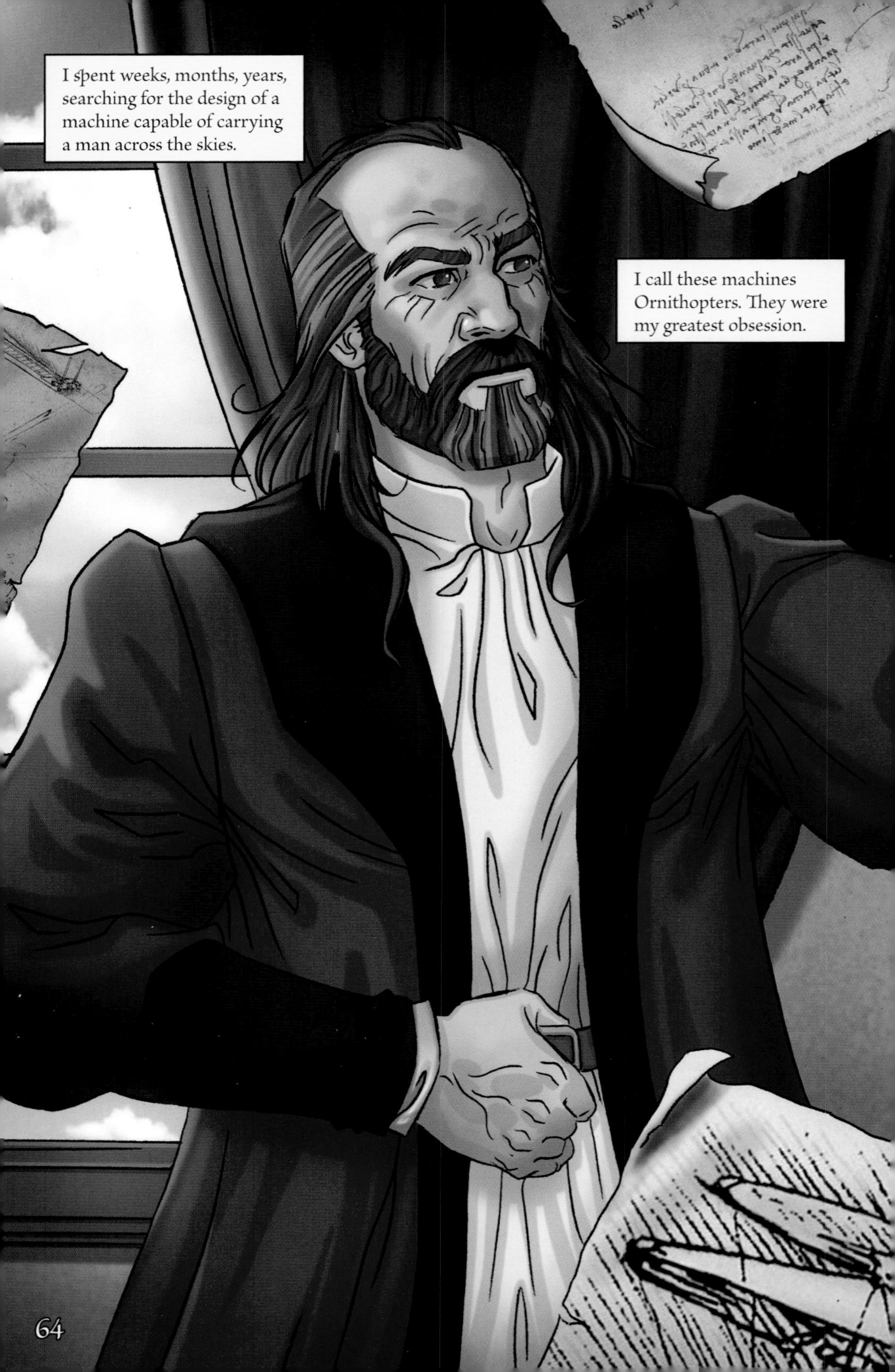
I spent weeks, months, years, searching for the design of a machine capable of carrying a man across the skies.
I call these machines Ornithopters. They were my greatest obsession.

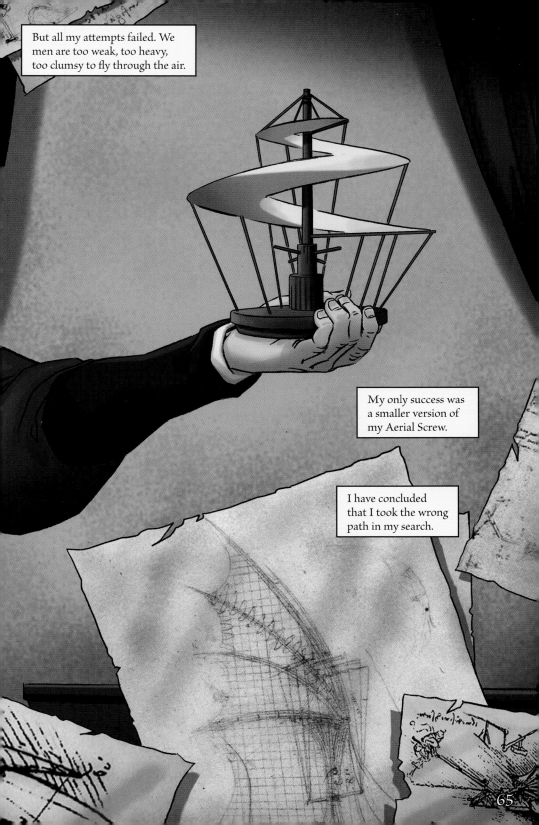

But all my attempts failed. We men are too weak, too heavy, too clumsy to fly through the air.

My only success was a smaller version of my Aerial Screw.

I have concluded that I took the wrong path in my search.

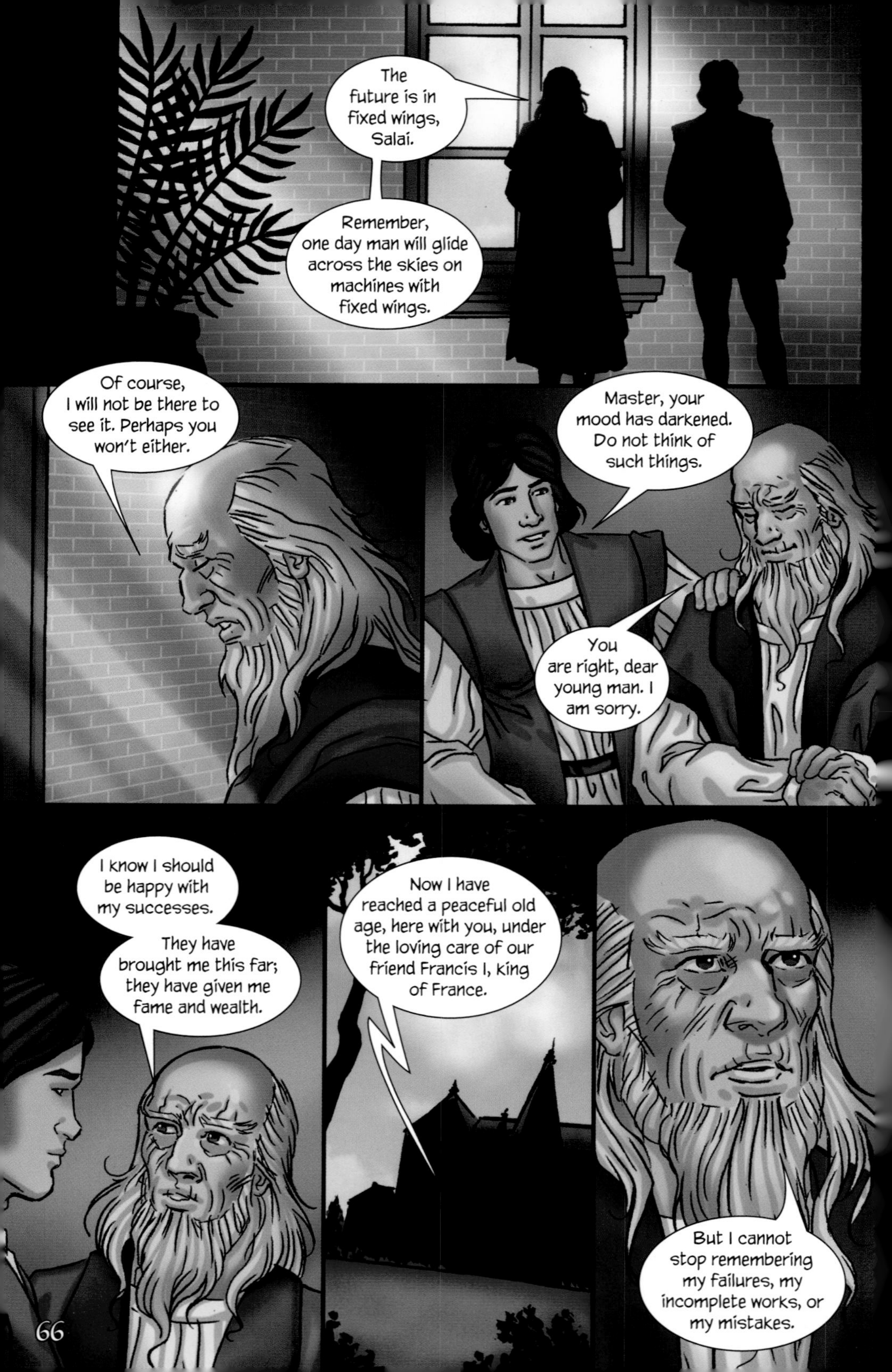

The future is in fixed wings, Salai.
Remember, one day man will glide across the skies on machines with fixed wings.
Of course, I will not be there to see it. Perhaps you won't either.
Master, your mood has darkened. Do not think of such things.
You are right, dear young man. I am sorry.
I know I should be happy with my successes.
They have brought me this far; they have given me fame and wealth.
Now I have reached a peaceful old age, here with you, under the loving care of our friend Francis I, king of France.
But I cannot stop remembering my failures, my incomplete works, or my mistakes.

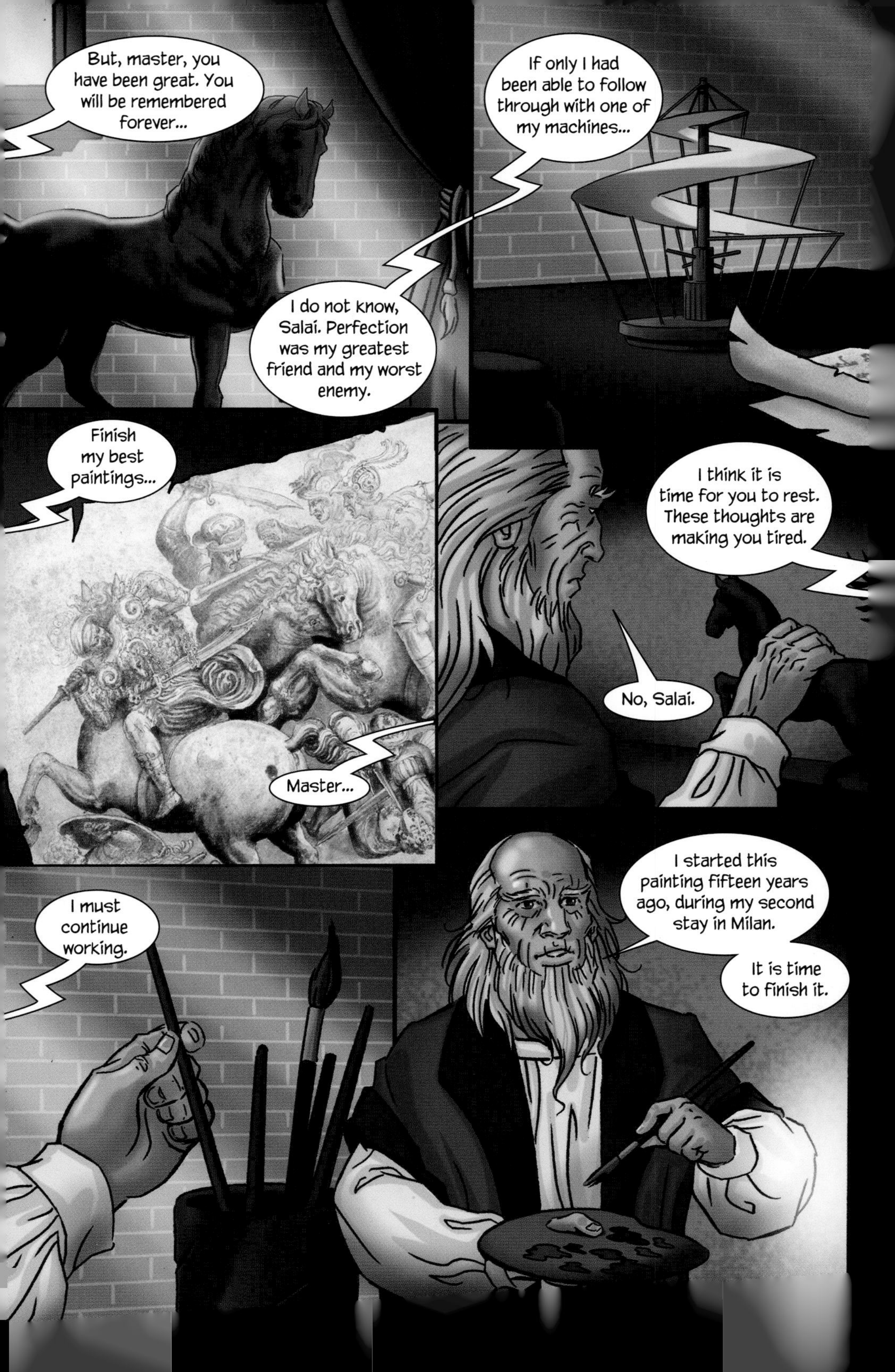

But, master, you have been great. You will be remembered forever...
I do not know, Salai. Perfection was my greatest friend and my worst enemy.
If only I had been able to follow through with one of my machines...
Finish my best paintings...
Master...
I think it is time for you to rest. These thoughts are making you tired.
No, Salai.
I must continue working.
I started this painting fifteen years ago, during my second stay in Milan.
It is time to finish it.

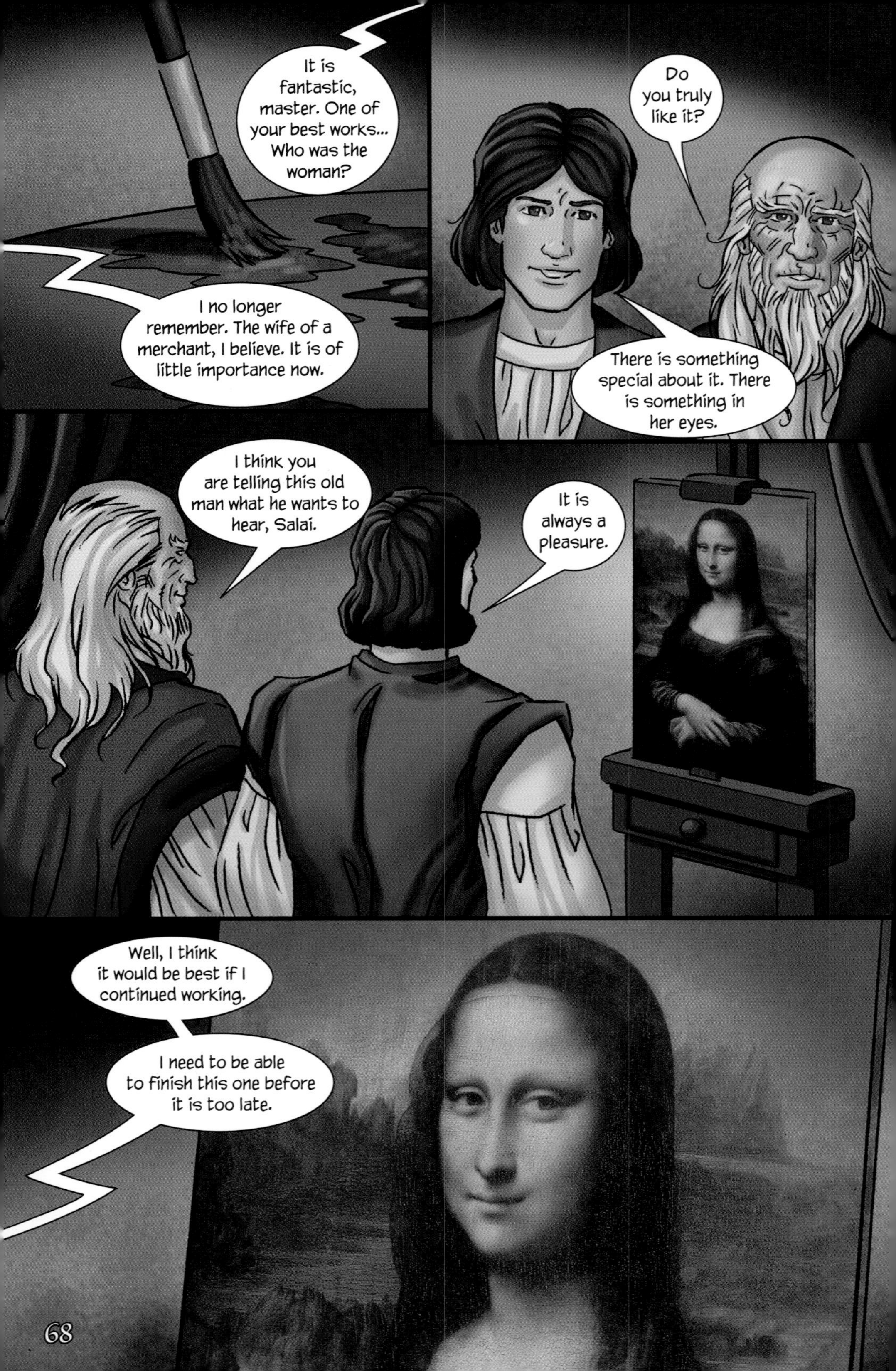
It is fantastic, master. One of your best works... Who was the woman?
I no longer remember. The wife of a merchant, I believe. It is of little importance now.
Do you truly like it?
There is something special about it. There is something in her eyes.
I think you are telling this old man what he wants to hear, Salai.
It is always a pleasure.
Well, I think it would be best if I continued working.
I need to be able to finish this one before it is too late.

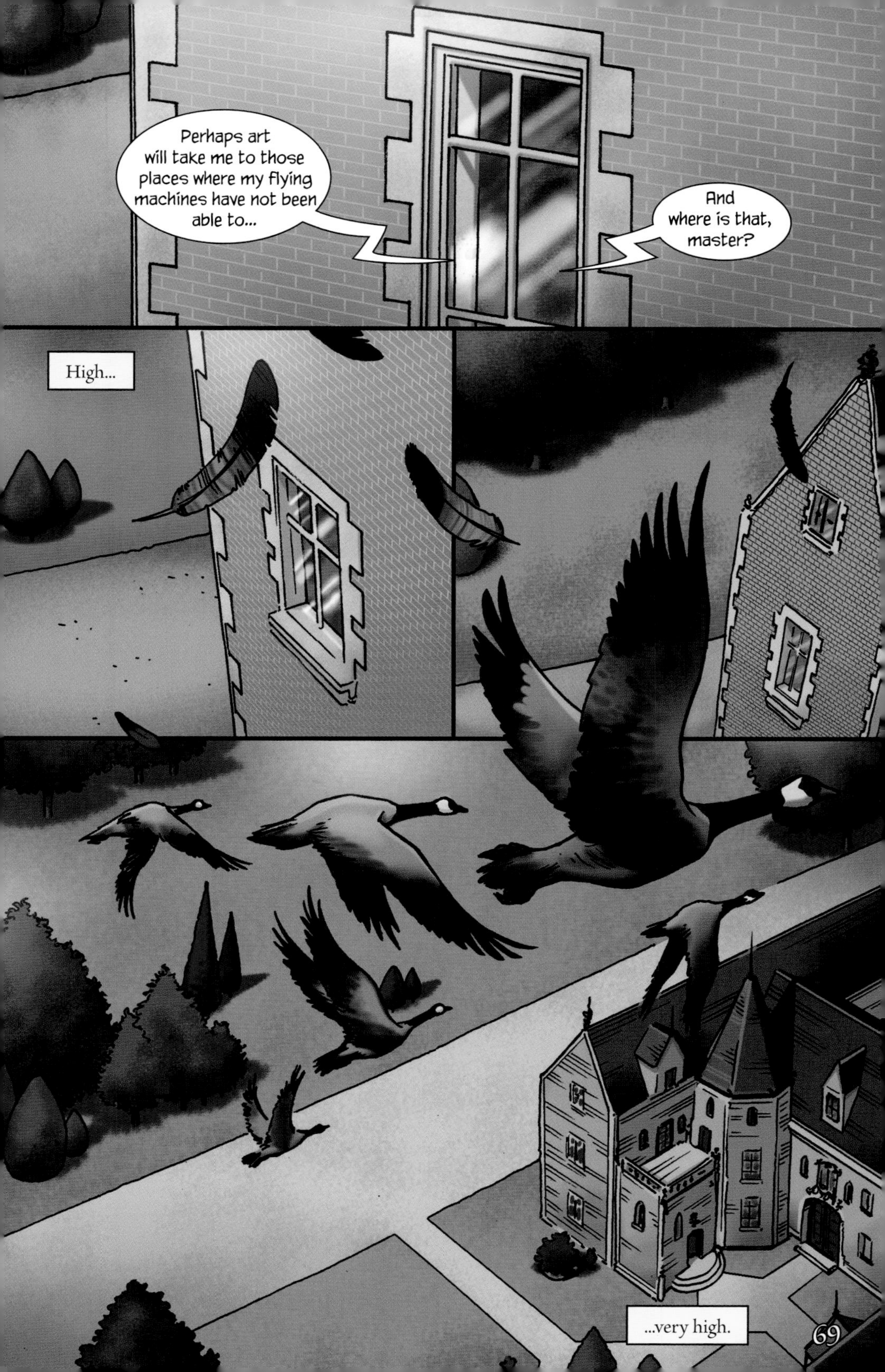
Perhaps art will take me to those places where my flying machines have not been able to...
And where is that, master?
High...
...very high.

TIMELINE
1452-1519

1452	1460s	1470s	1480s
Leonardo da Vinci is born on April 15, the son of Piero and Caterina, in the village of Vinci. There he spends all of his childhood.	Between 1466 and 1469, da Vinci lives in Florence along with his father. In this city he becomes an apprentice in Verrocchio's workshop.	Da Vinci's first dated drawing is from August 5, 1473. The detailed angel in Verrocchio's *Baptism of Christ* highlights his skills, and he goes on to paint the *Annunciation*. Both works are currently in Florence.	In 1481 da Vinci receives his first commission from the monks of San Donato, The *Adoration of the Magi*. In 1482 he moves to the court of Ludovico of Milan. He begins to paint *The Virgin of the Rocks*.

1490s	1500s	1510s	1519

In 1495 da Vinci is commissioned with a mural for the dining hall of Santa María delle Grazie, in Milan. As a result, he creates one of his masterpieces, *The Last Supper*. In 1499 he abandons Milan, following the fall of Ludovico.

The start of the new century finds da Vinci back in Florence, where he serves Cesare Borgia as an architect and military engineer. In 1503 he begins work on *The Battle of Anghiari*, at the Palazzo Vecchio. Around 1504, between trips from Florence to Milan, he begins painting *The Mona Lisa*. In 1508 he once again moves to Milan.

In 1513 da Vinci leaves Milan for the second and last time. He goes to Rome with money from Giuliano de Medici. In 1516 he heads to France with his apprentice. He works under the protection of King Francis I.

Da Vinci dies on May 2 in Clos Lucé, on the Loire River. He is buried in the church of Saint-Florentin.

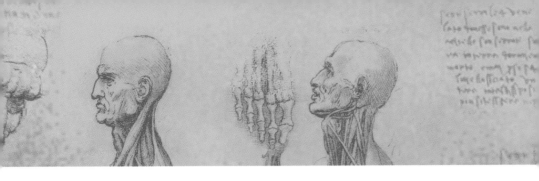

WHO WAS LEONARDO DA VINCI?

Leonardo da Vinci is known as a true Renaissance man, a figure who during his life embodied the spirit of his time. Curious about nature and a skilled student of the mechanics of the world around him, da Vinci stood out in the arts, engineering, human anatomy, biology, and many other fields.

Da Vinci was born on April 15, 1452, to Piero Fruosino and a peasant called Caterina in the city of Vinci. Little is known about his early years. What is certain is that he lived with his mother until the age of five, at which point he went to live with his father in 1457. During his childhood he received some informal education in mathematics, geometry, and Latin.

In 1466 he moved to Florence and became an apprentice in the workshop of Andrea di Cione, known as Verrocchio. There Leonardo first studied painting, but also chemistry, ironwork, engineering, and carpentry, among other manual skills. At the age of 20, Leonardo had already obtained the title of master, and it is believed that between 1476 and 1481 he had his own workshop in Florence.

In 1482 he moved to Milan to serve Duke Ludovico Sforza. There he produced some of his most renowned works, such as *The Last Supper*. At the same time, he developed different engineering projects for the city and designed the *Gran Cavallo*, a giant horse that he never managed to complete. He left Milan in 1499, following the French invasion.

In 1503 he served Cesare Borgia, the son of Pope Alexander VI, and traveled throughout Italy with him. He again settled in Milan in 1508, but he would leave this city once more in 1513. In 1516 he served King Francis I of France, who took him under his protection and provided him a home in Clos Luce, until his death on May 2, 1519.

LEONARDO AND THE MOVIES

The life of Leonardo da Vinci does not appear in many movies; it only made it to the small screen in an Italian made-for-television film produced during the 1970s. More recently, in 2013, the series *Da Vinci's Demons* was released, which follows the steps of a young Leonardo in Florence, as he becomes an artist and inventor. But the series departs from historical fact and focuses more on fantasy.

Despite this, many films, books, and elements of pop culture capture his work and his character in a different way. The most famous of these works is the novel *The Da Vinci Code*, by Dan Brown, which was adapted to film in 2006, with Tom Hanks playing the role of the expert symbologist Robert Langdon. The plot revolves around the unveiling of a series of clues that da Vinci may have left in his works and which guide Langdon to the discovery of a great secret.

Da Vinci and other Renaissance geniuses gave their names to the famous Teenage Mutant Ninja Turtles. Leonardo, Donatello, Michelangelo, and Rafael were four mutant turtles who, trained in the secrets of martial arts by a mutant rat, fight crime in New York City. These characters appeared in two recent films, in 2014 and 2016.

Leonardo da Vinci has also made an appearance as a secondary character in the video-game series *Assassin's Creed*. In the second installment of the game, set in Renaissance Florence, Leonardo helps the main character with his weapon inventions and designs.

ITALY AND THE RENAISSANCE

The intellectuals of the Renaissance coined the term "the Middle Ages" to define the historical period between the fall of Greece and Rome and the rediscovery of its artistic and philosophical ideals, at the beginning of the 15th century. For people of the Renaissance, the Middle Ages had been a period of cultural darkness, dominated by feudal power and strict religious rules, that needed to be put behind them.

The early scholars of the Renaissance were those who formed the movement called humanism. Their interest centered around all the expressions and successes of human nature and emphasized the dignity of man. This was the direct opposite of the life of punishment and suffering that, according to them, was characteristic of the Middle Ages.

This movement was started by scholars who, unlike what had occurred up to that point, did not belong to the church. Italy was the first place in Europe where humanism developed, with people such as the poets Dante Alighieri and Petrarch. However, the turning point for the evolution of humanism was the fall of the Eastern Roman Empire, in 1453, to the Ottoman Empire. Many scholars from its capital, Constantinople, arrived in Italy, bringing with them books and manuscripts about classic Greek traditions. In this way, European scholars were able to recover the classical heritage, the beginnings of their civilization.

Humanism sought to recover from those texts the wisdom and human spirit that had been lost, causing a break with the strict way of life set by the religious orders. The movement attempted to inspire curiosity about the world, rather than the blind acceptance of religious ideas. Humanists showed, above all, a strong belief in the possibilities opening up to people through critical thinking and creativity.

In this way, humanism proposed a "rebirth" of the classical spirit, which was primarily expressed in the field of the arts. The Renaissance artists used the beauty ideals of the Greek classics. But they also added new discoveries and technical advances, such as perspective and mathematical proportions. This made paintings of the time extremely realistic. Art came to be considered a branch of science, not so different from mathematics and biology. In this respect, Leonardo da Vinci was a true "Renaissance man," who displayed better than any other a mastery of all of these fields of knowledge.

The city of Florence was one of the main places for the development of Renaissance art and to this day displays many pieces of art developed there during that period. Wealthy merchant families, such as the Medici, lived in Florence and commissioned the best artists of that time to produce sculptures. These commissions, such as statues of the city's patron saints, were displayed on churches, palaces, and monasteries. The most renowned artists had workshops in Florence, as was the case with Verrocchio, Leonardo's master.

Alongside Leonardo, other distinguished figures of Renaissance art included Michelangelo and Rafael. These two artists' masterpieces can be found in the Vatican. The works of Michelangelo that stand out are the *Pietà,* a sculpture of the Virgin Mary holding the body of Jesus, and the ceiling fresco of the Sistine Chapel. Rafael's genius, and perhaps a large part of the Renaissance spirit, can be seen in the fresco of the *School of Athens.* It illustrates the most important thinkers of the Greek tradition who influenced the humanists.

GLOSSARY

abandon (uh-BAN-duhn)—to leave forever; to give up

anatomy (uh-NA-tuh-mee)—the study of the human body

catapult (KAT-uh-puhlt)—a weapon used to hurl rocks, liquid, or other items at an enemy

client (KLY-uhnt)—a customer

commission (kuh-MI-shun)—money for work done

composition (kom-puh-ZISH-uhn)—the combining of parts to make a whole; in art, a painting's composition describes how the different parts have been arranged to make a complete work

curiosity (kyur-ee-AHSS-i-tee)—something that shows interest

delay (di-LAY)—to be late, to make someone or something late, or to put something off until later

dense (DENSS)—crowded or thick

divine (dih-VINE)—having to do with gods

engineering (en-juh-NEER-ing)—using science to design and build things

fresco (FREHSK-oh)—a large picture painted on wet plaster

Golden Ratio (GOHLD-en RAY-shee-oh)—a compositional rule in art that splits a work of art into an appealing mathematical proportion; also called divine proportion and rule of thirds, da Vinci's paintings are especially known for following this rule

hydraulics (HYE-drawl-iks)—branch of physics that studies the movement of liquids

inherit (in-HER-it)—to receive a physical possessions from one's parents

lock (LOK)—an area of water with gates at both ends; locks help boats move from one water level to another

modern (MOD-urn)—up-to-date or new in style

mortar (MOR-tur)—a short cannon that fires shells or rockets high in the air

mural (MYU-ruhl)—a painting on a wall

ocher (OH-ker)—yellow or reddish-yellow iron ore or other earth material used to color paint

patron (PAY-tron)—someone who supports an artist or writer

pose (POHZE)—a body positioned or arranged so that it can be photographed, painted, or drawn

prosper (PROSS-pur)—to be successful

pyramidal (PIHR-uh-mid-uhl)—something in the shape of a pyramid or triangle

reputation (rep-yoo-TAY-shuhn)—a person's character as judged by other people

scaffold (SKAF-uhld)—temporary framework or set of platforms used to support workers and their materials off the ground

Sfumato (sfu-MAH-toh)—Italian word meaning toned down or blurred; a painting technique created by Leonardo da Vinci, by applying several layers of paint to create depth

surpass (sur-PASS)—to be better, greater, or stronger than another person or thing

technique (tek-NEEK)—a method or way of doing something that requires skill

DISCUSSION QUESTIONS

1. Find examples of humanism, the strong belief in critical thinking and creativity, in the text. Explain why this example fits within the humanist movement.

2. Of all the different kinds of art that da Vinci practiced, which do you think he preferred the most? Which kind do you believe was his best?

3. Why do you think da Vinci found it so difficult to finish some of his works? Was it his fault or was it due to what was happening around him?

WRITING PROMPTS

1. Choose one of da Vinci's paintings that appear in the graphic novel and write a description. Share it with your classmates, without saying which one you chose, to see if they can identify it.

2. Imagine that you are one of Verrocchio's apprentices in his workshop. Write a diary entry and describe what you did there.

3. Write about the confrontation between da Vinci and Michelangelo, but from Michelangelo's point of view.

ABOUT THE AUTHOR

Diego Agrimbau, from Buenos Aires, Argentina, has written more than a dozen graphic novels for various publishing houses around the world. He has won multiple awards, among them the 2005 Prix Utopiales for *Bertold's Bubble*, the 2009 Premio Planeta DeAgostini for Comic Books for *Planet Extra*, and the 2011 Premio Dibujando entre Culturas for *The Desert Robots*. He's currently a contributor to *Fierro* magazine and writes "Los Canillitas" comic scripts for the newspaper *Tiempo Argentino*.

ABOUT THE ILLUSTRATOR

Diego Aballay is a Professor of Fine Arts with Drawing orientation and graduated from the School of Fine Artes of La Plata National University. He studied comic book drawing with masters Raúl Fortín and Alberto Salinas, and he studied illustration and color with Juan Bobillo and Marcelo Sosa at Sotano Blanco school. He has published his comic books in Argentina, Chile, and USA. He has also made drawings and storyboards for advertising. He participated in three animation movies, among them *Patoruzito* and *Condor Crux*. For the last 21 years, he gave workshops on comic book drawing for kids, teenagers, and adults.

READ MORE

Ciovacco, Justine. *Leonardo da Vinci: Genius of the Italian Renaissance*. Britannica Beginner Bios. New York: Britannica Educational Publishing, 2015.

DeMocker, Michael. *Leonardo. Brush with Greatness*. Kennett Square, Pa.: Purple Toad Publishing, 2017.

Zaczek, Iain. *Leonardo da Vinci*. Great Artists. New York: Gareth Stevens Publishing, 2015.

INTERNET SITES

Use Facthound to find Internet sites related to this book.

Visit *www.facthound.com*

Just type in 9781515791638 and go!

 Check out projects, games and lots more at
www.capstonekids.com

INDEX